NOT ETCHED IN STONE

Essays on Ritual Memory, Soul, and Society

I0130413

Edited by

Marie A. Conn
Thérèse McGuire

University Press of America,® Inc.
Lanham · Boulder · New York · Toronto · Plymouth, UK

Copyright © 2007 by
University Press of America,® Inc.
4501 Forbes Boulevard
Suite 200
Lanham, Maryland 20706
UPA Acquisitions Department (301) 459-3366

Estover Road
Plymouth PL6 7PY
United Kingdom

Library of Congress Control Number: 2007922240
ISBN-13: 978-0-7618-3702-2 (paperback : alk. paper)
ISBN-10: 0-7618-3702-7 (paperback : alk. paper)

⊖™ The paper used in this publication meets the minimum
requirements of American National Standard for Information
Sciences—Permanence of Paper for Printed Library Materials,
ANSI Z39.48—1984

This book is dedicated, with love and gratitude, to

Bob, Kelsey and Anders
Julia and Leon
Mr. and Mrs. Victor DeCesare
Our families
Our students at Chestnut Hill
The Sisters of St. Joseph of Chestnut Hill
The Resilient Children of the American Foster Care System
All the World's Children

And to the memory of

Alice and Ira Conn
Regis Duffy, OFM
Bill and Pauline Lonnquist
John and Anna McGuire
Mark Porter, Sr.

And, to paraphrase James Joyce,

To all those who turn back the stones of death with the living
waters of peace and reconciliation

Contents

Contents

Introduction

A few years ago, some of us at Chestnut Hill College decided to work together on a book of essays. The result was *Balancing the Scales*, published by University Press of America. The whole enterprise proved so rewarding that we decided to gather professors again for a second volume. *Not Etched in Stone* is the fruit of that decision. The essays come from professors in a variety of disciplines, and approach the theme of "Ritual Memory, Soul, and Society" across a wide spectrum of time and experience.

The essays fall naturally into three parts: Marie Conn and Therese McGuire take an historical approach; Margie Thompson and Barbara Lonnquist use various forms of literature as their starting point; and Nancy DeCesare, Sara Kitchen, and Nancy Porter make contemporary applications in their particular fields.

In the first chapter, Marie Conn, a theologian, looks at water (feminine) and stone (masculine) as vehicles for ritual memory. Once again going back to the earliest days of human history, Conn will trace examples of water and stone through the centuries and in various cultures. In the present day, one of the most powerful examples is Maya Lin's memorial to the martyrs of the Civil Rights Movement found outside the offices of the Southern Poverty Law Center in Montgomery, Alabama. The new World War II memorial in Washington, DC, is the most recent example of water, stone, and memory.

In her chapter, Therese McGuire, SSJ, an art historian, includes an investigation of the aesthetic principles of the Middle Ages which led up to and encouraged the advancement of the beautiful stained glass windows of the Gothic cathedrals of Europe, of the British Isles, and eventually of the Gothic style cathedrals in North America.

> The nature of light is such that its whole beauty is based not
> on number, not on measure, and not on weight or anything

> else like it, but on sight...light makes things beautiful and
> shows their beauty in the highest degree. [Grosseteste,
> *Commentary on Pseudo-Dionysius' Divine Names*, IV, p. 230.]

In the Middle Ages Abbot Suger ushered in a new concept of the beauty of
light streaming through stained glass windows to create an atmosphere of
heavenly light reflected on the "sacred stones" of the walls of Gothic Cathedrals.
Such beauty was to be regarded by the faithful as God's grace illuminating the
soul with an extraordinary variety of colorful beauty.

Margie Thompson, SSJ, an artist, compares Julian of Norwich and Etty
Hillesum, two women mystics whose lives were in danger, Julian from the
Black Plague and the Inquisition; Etty from the Holocaust. Themes include
embodied prayer and prayer through writing; parallel messages in Julian's
refrain "all shall be well," and Etty's "life is beautiful." Space figures
prominently in both stories: Julian the anchoress gets walled in but listens to the
stories of her people from her window on the world becoming the listening heart
of Norwich. Etty's precious writer's desk serves as her cloister cell while she
worked out her life issues in her diaries. As the Nazis moved into Amsterdam,
Etty's space progressively narrows terminating in the gas chambers in
Auschwitz. In the internment camp of Westerbork, Etty prays to become the
"thinking heart of the barracks."

Literature is also at the heart of the chapter by Barbara Lonnquist, a scholar
of English. Barbara looks at the last book of *Finnegan's Wake*, in which the Irish
Catholics believed they were paralyzed, turned into stone. The symbolic mother
and father are river and mountain. Mother Ireland was the water woman. In
1922 Ireland didn't really experience independence, since there was too much
control by the church. There is a play on spirit and stone: pneumatic becomes
rheumatic wheels. Stone, dust, and clay are contrasted with water: water is
laughter and openness; stones gets broken apart by water.

Drawing on her years working in the field of foster care, Nancy DeCesare,
IHM, looks at the issue of providing comprehensive mental health services to
children and adolescents in the American foster care system as a primary
intervention for maintaining and supporting positive psychological growth and
inner healing. A review of child welfare literature reveals a mental health system
that is ill funded, fragmented and problematic. Children and adolescents with
severe mental health problems are often moved from placement to placement
without access to ongoing mental health services. This chapter, then, reviews the
literature on the problems of the child welfare system with regard to mental
health services and discusses model programs for providing comprehensive
assessments and ongoing care. The primary focus on the development of access
to mental health services combined with many social supports for foster care
children will enhance their wellbeing.

Sara Kitchen, a sociologist, notes that we seem to have hardened our hearts
to the deaths of children. High infant mortality rates have led to a human rights
focus on breast feeding. But then we face the problem of the lack of clean water

and also have to acknowledge that breast feeding transmits AIDS from mother to child. We have the enlightenment but are not adequately addressing this. 9-11 has been over-memorialized. Most children do not have grave markers; in New York City, 90% of those buried in paupers' graves are children. Sara's essay looks at this important and complex topic from a variety of angles.

Finally, Nancy Porter, a psychologist, looks at the concept of enlightenment and traces changing understandings of the purpose of therapy in the history of psychology. Enlightenment and self-actualization will be examined through the lenses of Jung, Maslow, and Rogers. Today, there seems to be an emphasis on the "fix-it" for most people, but "the talking cure" for the wealthy. By going to back to premodern Western views of the essence of the human, postmodern psychology challenges the completeness of science and objective thought as the ultimate method of investigation and explanation.

Chapter One

From the Rock Came Living Water: Stone and Water as Vehicles of Ritual Memory

Marie A. Conn

Introduction

In Montgomery, Alabama, near the intersection of Rosa Parks Avenue and W. Jefferson Davis Avenue, not far from the State Capitol and just a block away from the Dexter Avenue King Memorial Baptist Church, Maya Lin's powerful Civil Rights Memorial sits outside the offices of the Southern Poverty Law Center. As she did in designing the Vietnam War Memorial in Washington, DC, Lin here opts for a simple blending of water, stone, and names. The memorial has two main components: a nine-foot-high, forty-foot-long bowed stone wall, and a low, round table of smooth black granite. (Figure 1, page 2.) The memorial evokes Dr. Martin Luther King Jr.'s "I Have a Dream" speech; the words he used, paraphrasing the bible, "Until justice rolls down like water and righteousness like a mighty stream," are inscribed in the wall.

Carved into the top of the table are pivotal events of the Civil Rights Movement of the 1950s and 60s, as well as the names of forty people who gave their lives in that struggle, with a brief description of how and when each died. Water bubbles up from the center of the table and spills gently across its surface. Lin hoped her use of water would be soothing. "Inviting to the touch, the water in [this work] leaves a physical trace on those who venture to feel the names and numbers. . . . Lin's use of water also predicts the demise of the memorial itself, as centuries of running water will eventually soften the stone, turning it back into earth."[1]

A few years ago, a colleague and I traveled through the South with forty adult students, visiting sites connected with the Civil Rights Movement in Virginia, Georgia, and Alabama. While it would be difficult to compare the impact of the many places on our itinerary, Maya Lin's memorial in Montgomery ranks among the most moving.

This essay will examine the ancient and enduring symbolism of water and stone, seeking to discover why they have for millennia been used as vehicles of ritual memory. Other examples of the use of water and stone in contemporary memorials both in the United States and abroad will then be explored.

Stone as Ancient Symbol
> Up from the bed of the river
> God scooped the clay,
> And by the bank of the river
> He kneeled him down;
> And there the great God Almighty
> Who lit the sun and fixed it in the sky,
> Who flung the stars to the most far corner of the night,
> Who rounded the earth in the middle of his hand;
> This Great God,
> Like a mammy bending over his baby,
> Kneeled down in the dust
> Toiling over a lump of clay
> Till he shaped it in his own image;
> Then into it he blew the breath of life,
> And man became a living soul.
> Amen. Amen.[2]

Water and stone are two of the most pervasive and powerful symbols in human history. Many creation stories show deities using either or both of these materials as the stuff out of which humanity is created. James Weldon Johnson's dynamic interpretation of Genesis 2 paints a vivid picture of the God of the bible stooping down by the river and using a mixture of earth and water to shape the first earth creature. And Genesis itself borrows from the Greek story of Prometheus.

Prometheus, whose name means forethought, and his brother, Epimetheus, afterthought, were the grandsons of the Titan Oceanus, the son of Kronos' brother, Iapetos. Prometheus had helped Zeus in the war against Kronos and the Titans, while his brother had remained neutral, since he could not make up his mind. As a reward for Prometheus' help, Zeus charged the brothers with the creation of earthly creatures. Epimetheus was to make the animals and humans, while Prometheus would put on the finishing touches. But Epimetheus made the animals first and, in so doing, used up all the gifts the gods had given them, gifts of speed, strength, fur, feathers, and so on. Then Epimetheus made a mold in the shape of the gods. Prometheus filled the mold with a mixture of water and clay and the first human was created.[3]

A related story tells of the importance of both water and stone in the development of humanity. Water in this version is the means used by the gods to destroy the wicked inhabitants of earth, while stone provides the building material for a new race of humans.

In the most ancient of days, Time begot the Ages. The Golden Age, the Age of Kronos, was a time of natural morality, with no war and endless spring. This was followed by the Silver Age, the age of Zeus, when seasons developed and there was need to toil. During the Bronze Age, people became more militant but were not yet corrupt. During the Iron Age, however, the earth was filled with every sort of wickedness, treachery, and violence. Life was corrupted by private ownership of land, commerce by sea, and the exploitation of the earth.

Finally, disgusted, Zeus decided to destroy the human race. He sent rain and enlisted his brother, Poseidon, to send floods. It happened that Prometheus' son, Deucalion, had married Pyrrha, the daughter of Epimetheus and Pandora. Prometheus warned the couple to build a large chest; he spared them because of their virtue and piety. After nine days and nights, the chest came to rest on Mount Parnassus and the couple, emerging, gave thanks to the gods. Realizing they were alone, they consulted the Oracle at Themis. She instructed them to throw the bones of their mother behind them. They came to understand that their mother was the earth and her bones were the stones. So they walked along, throwing stones over their shoulders. The stones thrown by Deucalion became men and those thrown by Pyrrha became women. Thus, a hardier human race, more able to withstand temptation and wickedness, was born.[4]

This image of stones as the bones of Mother Earth is not unique. Sacred stones have been known from earliest times; stones have long been used as sacred objects, as memorials, or as boundary markers.[5] The worship of meteors, stones fallen from heaven, was quite common; "they were thought of as a symbolic manifestation of a connection between heaven and earth. . . . Because of their hardness and immutability, stones are frequently associated with eternal, unchanging, divine powers and are thought of as a manifestation of concentrated energy."[6] Meteorites were thought to grant fertility and to bring rain, insuring both children and a good harvest.

In many cultures, stone is viewed as a primal cause and also a burden. Stone is marked by durability, firmness, and permanence, a representation of the potency of human life. Because it is an unreceptive substance, firm and resisting impression, stone is a symbol of the spirit.[7] In Greek mythology, after Chronos, fearing being overthrown by one of his children, has swallowed five newborns, his wife Rhea bundles a stone in blankets and hands the "infant" to her husband; thus Rhea saves the infant Zeus.

The worship of sacred stones constituted one of the most general and ancient forms of religion; but among no other people was this worship so important as among the Semites. The religion of the nomads of Syria and Arabia was summarized by Clement of Alexandria in the single statement, "The Arabs worship the stone, and all the data afforded by Arabian authors regarding the pre-Islamic faith confirm his words. The sacred stone (*nuisb*; plural, *ansab*) is a characteristic and indispensable feature in an ancient Arabian place of worship.

Among the Canaanites, as the Old Testament abundantly proves, the worship of *mazzebot* was common; while with regard to the Phenicians [sic], Herodotus states that the temple of Melkart at Tyre contained two sacred pillars. In like manner, two columns were erected for the temples at Paphos and Hierapolis, and a conical stone was worshiped as a symbol of Astarte in her temple in the former city.[8]

Upright stones used as grave markers "signify protection of the dead from hostile powers; they were also sometimes thought to be the place where the energy or soul of the deceased continued to live."[9] In Genesis, we read of Jacob erecting a funerary stela on Rachel's grave (Gn. 35:20); a stela also commemorates the pact between Jacob and the Aramaeans (Gn. 31:43ff). Earlier in the story, Jacob, while fleeing Esau, is visited by God in a dream. Jacob takes his stone pillow, makes it a pillar, anoints it with oil, and calls it *beit-El* (Bethel), the "house of God," apparently symbolizing God's presence.[10]

Stones were a natural choice for altars, and were commonly associated with trees and springs in sacred places. "The notion that a certain stone deserved special veneration as the *omphalos*, or navel of the universe, is common not only among the early Greeks but among other peoples as well."[11] The biblical hero David defeats Goliath with five stones, the five powers of perfection or wisdom. Christianity used stones as a symbol of the strength needed by the martyrs; Cephas' name is changed to Peter, the rock, the cornerstone. Peter in his letter likewise assures us that we will be built up like living stones to be a spiritual house (1 Pt. 2:5).

In Indonesia, stones are considered the progenitors of the human race: first man was born from a stone. The Greeks placed quadrilateral pillars, called herms after Hermes, whose name means stone and who is the god of crossroads, at all their crossroads. Hermes guided travelers, acted as the messenger of the gods, and guided souls to the Underworld. In Norwegian lore, memorial stones are proportionate in size to the importance of the person memorialized. The person is considered to live in the memorial monument, accepting the sacrifices described before death.[12] The stone circles in England marked the spot where the king stood surrounded by his nobles. Stone heaps were often used as monuments commemorating remarkable events. At Stonehenge, where thirty grand pillars are thought by many scholars to be a gigantic timekeeper, any water which touched the stones became a remedy for sickness and wounds, an early fusion of stone with water.[13]

Stones, with their hardness and durability, represent cohesion, the harmonious reconciliation with the self. Stones are not subject to the biological laws of change, decay, death, and disintegration, so the whole stone represents unity and strength. Stones fallen from heaven explain the origin of life. "In volcanic eruptions, air turned to fire, fire became 'water' and 'water' changed to stone; hence stone constitutes the first solid form of the creative rhythm—the sculpture of essential movement, and the petrified music of creation."[14] Stones can also signify truths which are particularly hard to grasp.[15]

Like all symbols, stone has its dark side. Scripturally, stones sometimes denote hardheartedness or insensibility. Ezekiel, in a passage rendered even more potent in this day of nearly-routine heart transplants, assures us that God will take out our stony hearts and give us true hearts of flesh in their place (Ezek. 36:26).

Water as Ancient Symbol

Myths tell us that water has been important to humans from the most ancient times as a significant element of the universal order. Water is often tied mysteriously to the birth of first humans or the destiny of a god. In some myths, water is a product of divine action. In others, water is itself generative. In the Greek system, for example, Earth gives birth to Heaven and Pontus (the sea) and then mates with both these male principles. The first child of Earth and Heaven is Okeanos, a fresh-water river, who becomes the father of all springs and rivers. Thus the transcendent sky-god, Heaven, remains somehow immanent in the world.[16]

Since water is essential to life, it is often identified with life-bearing forces; the great symbol of truth and the eternal reality; the source of all revelation.[17] In Celtic myth, running water is associated with knowledge and inspiration. At the Buddha's birth, two pure streams of water fell down from heaven upon his head.[18] Waters are often bound up with divine powers, either as deities themselves or as the abode of spirits. Because of its unformed mass, water "symbolizes the abundance of all possibilities or the primeval beginning of all that exists, the *material* prima."[19]

In the Vedas, water is referred to as mâtritamâh (the most maternal) because, in the beginning, everything was like a sea without light. In India, this element is generally regarded as the preserver of life, circulating throughout the whole of nature, in the form of rain, sap, milk and blood. Limitless and immortal, the waters are the beginning and the end of all things on earth.[20]

"The force of water rushing in a wadi after a rainstorm was for the people of the Near East a symbol of the majesty and power of the divinity. An abundance of water was, and still is, for the peoples of parched lands a symbol of happiness and divine blessing."[21] Many cultures associate water with healing and immortality, the "water of life." Thetis, for example, in order to give her son Achilles eternal life, plunges him into the Styx (only the heel by which she held him remained vulnerable, the origin of our "Achilles' heel").[22]

Water, a source of both good and evil, symbolizes cleansing, the cosmic mind, healing, the subconscious, truth, and wisdom, an expression of the vital potential of the psyche.[23] Water is a purifier of the dead and of those who mourn them. As an agent of purification, water bathes, dissolves, carries away material filth; this leads to a use of water to purify from sin. In the Old Testament, water is used for purifying lepers, at times of sickness, for cleaning utensils, and for cleansing anyone defiled by touching an unclean body (Lev. 15:16-22, 27).[24] Since washing with water helped bring about a higher degree of purity, the priests whose duties took them into the inner shrine of the Temple were obliged first to wash their hands and feet.[25]

Biblically, purification was sometimes done with lustral water. The Book of Numbers (19:1-22) gives minute instructions for the preparation and use of lustral water in which the ashes of a red heifer were mixed. This water was used to remove legal uncleanness. Sometimes the subject of purification was required to wash his hands and feet or some other part of the body. Thus Aaron and his sons had to purify themselves before entering the tabernacle (Ex. 30:18-20).[26]

The blessing of water as a symbol of life and purification is important in the Byzantine liturgy. Basil the Great ascribed the introduction of the blessing of water to ancient tradition.[27] The oldest evidence is found in Tertullian.[28] Among the Byzantines, water in the forms of whirlpool, sea, or flood was considered a symbol of destruction, while water was also used in pre-Christian fortune-telling procedures.[29]

Offering water as a libation is another ancient custom. During the morning service on each of the seven days of the Feast of Tabernacles (Sukkot), water from the pool of Siloam was carried in procession to the temple, where the water and some wine were poured out as libations.[30] After repeated defeats at the hands of the Philistines, Samuel commanded the Israelites to gather at Mizpeh and pour water on the ground before Yahweh (1 Sam. 7:5-6). In his dispute with the priests of Baal, Elijah poured water in the trench that surrounded the altar on Mount Carmel, presumably to ensure the effectiveness of his sacrifice (1 Kgs. 18:35).

An unusual use of water is found in the Book of Numbers and is referred to as the "water of bitterness." A priest poured water from the temple into an earthen vessel; this water was then mixed with dust from the temple floor. A woman who was suspected of being unfaithful to her husband was brought to the priest, who pronounced maledictions which he then wrote on a little scroll. The scroll was dissolved in the prepared water and the accused woman was obliged to drink the mixture (Num. 5:11-31).

In many cultures, water is considered an uncreated first principle, the source of all created things, the first of the five elements. Water is the female counterpart of the male, the stone. The water of life bestows immortality; it is the source of the sun's daily rebirth in fountains, rivers, and streams. Water takes the shape of the vessel that holds it.[31] All life comes from the waters. "Limitless and immortal, the waters are the beginning and the end of all things on earth."[32] Many myths describe the afterlife in places filled with rivers or lakes.[33]

Water has long been important and precious to the Jews. The first thing offered to a guest is water to wash the feet (Gn. 18:4; 24:32), and it is the duty of hospitality to offer water to strangers coming to the house or even just passing by (Gn. 24:17, 43). When the Israelites were wandering in the desert, the lack of water caused them to complain to Moses (Ex. 15:22-25; 17:1-7; Num. 20:1-13). The heroes of David's guard won distinction by procuring water for the king at the risk of their own lives (2 Sam. 23:16; 1 Chron. 11:17-18).[34]

The word water is also used biblically to express grief (Jer. 9:1, 18; Ps. 119:136). A misfortune of great magnitude, nearly impossible to comprehend, was likened to water (Lam. 3:54; Ps. 69:2; 124:4-5). The constant flow and unrest of water came to be seen as a symbol of numerous descendants (Num. 24:7); while God was sometimes referred to as the fountain of living water (Jer. 2:13).[35]

Waters evoke the universal gathering of potentialities. "Immersion in water signifies a return to the preformal state, with a sense of death and annihilation on the one hand, but of rebirth and regeneration on the other, since immersion intensifies the life-force."[36] In the Christian tradition, the fullest expression of the initiation ritual of baptism is through full immersion. Cosmically, this is the equivalent of being submerged in the flood and rising to a new life. The female symbol of water, with its transparency and depth, becomes the home of wisdom, as well as an image of fertility and birth. Water is thus the mediator between life and death, most clearly transitional between the ethereal elements of fire and air, and the solid element of earth. Cirlot, referring to the Greek belief that shades approaching the Underworld had to pay the ferryman Charon and cross the river Styx, refers to death as "the first mariner."[37]

The symbolism of water "is an expression of the vital potential of the psyche, of the struggles of the psychic depths to find a way of formulating a clear message comprehensible to the consciousness."[38] The Chinese philosopher Lao-Tse, considered the founder of the Taoist school, discusses water this way:

Water never rests, neither by day nor by night. When flowing above, it causes rain and dew. When flowing below, it forms streams and rivers. Water is outstanding in doing good. If a dam is raised against it, it stops. If way is made for it, it flows along that path. Hence it is said that it does not struggle. And yet it has no equal in destroying that which is strong and hard.[39]

Memorials in Water and Stone

On February 12, 1914, ground was broken in Washington, DC, for the Lincoln Memorial. Designed by Henry Bacon, with the famous colossal statue sculpted by Daniel Chester French, the memorial included the introduction of the Reflecting Pool, now so familiar to any visitor to the American capital. Since then, numerous other memorials in Washington and elsewhere have blended the ancient symbols of water and stone, giving people places of quiet and refreshment as they remember fallen heroes, tragic events, and key moments in history.[40]

FDR Memorial

The Franklin Delano Roosevelt Memorial is one of the most expansive memorials in the nation. Yet, its shade trees, waterfalls, statuary, and quiet alcoves create the feeling of a secluded garden rather than an imposing structure. The memorial is divided into four outdoor galleries, or rooms, one for each of FDR's terms in office. The rooms are defined by walls of red South Dakota granite and by ornamental plantings; quotations from FDR are carved into the

granite. Water cascades and quiet pools are present throughout. Each room con-
veys in its own way the spirit of this great man.[41]

Just west of Washington's Tidal Basin, in West Potomac Park, the FDR
Memorial honors the 32nd president of the United States. Although Lawrence
Halprin's ambitious design runs counter to Roosevelt's own wish for a simple
memorial, it is very popular with visitors.

The four "galleries" of the memorial tell the story of America's only four-
term president. These galleries—"The Early Years," "The Great Depression,"
"The Horrors of a World at War," and "Seeds of Peace"—combine water and
sculpture with plants and quotations to trace American history under FDR's
leadership.[42]

Approximately 100,000 gallons of water are recycled every minute through
the entire monument. There are 31,439 stones, totaling 6,000 tons, in the design.
The largest of these, "The Mother Stone" in room three, measures 29 feet by 6
feet.[43]

Korean War Veterans Memorial

On July 27, 1995, the Korean War Veterans Memorial in Washington, DC,
was dedicated. The memorial consists of a black granite wall, nineteen stainless
steel statues, and a Pool of Remembrance.

Designed by Louis Nelson, the wall consists of 41 panels. The mural, based
on computer-enhanced photographs, depicts Army, Navy, Marine Corps, Air
Force, and Coast Guard personnel. "The reflective quality of the Academy
Black Granite creates the image of a total of 38 statues, symbolic of the 38th
Parallel and the 38 months of the war. When viewed from afar, it also creates
the appearance of the mountain ranges of Korea."[44] Among the etchings are
supporting artillery, rescue helicopters, surgeons, nurses, ambulances, stretcher
bearers, chaplains of various denominations, radio communications, and other
elements critical to the combat effort.

The nineteen statues were sculpted by Frank Gaylord. They are more than
7' tall and include fourteen representatives of the Army, three Marines, and one
representative each from the Navy and the Air Force. They also depict the ethnic
diversity of the armed forces, with twelve Caucasians, three African Americans,
two Hispanics, and one each of Asian and Native American descent.[45]

The juniper bushes are meant to be symbolic of the rough terrain encountered in Korea, and the granite stripes of the obstacles overcome in war. The
Marines in column have the helmet chin straps fastened and helmet covers.
Three of the Army statues are wearing paratrooper boots and all equipment is
authentic from the Korean War era (when the war started most of the equipment
was WWII issue). Three of the statues are in the woods, so if you are at the flag-
pole looking through the troops, you can't tell how many there are, and could be
legions emerging from the woods. The statues are made of stainless steel, a reflective material that when seen in bright sunlight causes the figures to come to
life. The blowing ponchos give motion to the column, so you can feel them
walking up the hill with the cold winter wind at their backs, talking to one an-

other. At nighttime the fronts of the statues are illuminated with a special white light; the finer details of the sculpture are clearly seen and the ghosts appear.[46]

The Pool of Remembrance honors the dead, the missing, and the POWs from American and United Nations forces. The visitor walks out into the pool area on a peninsula symbolic of the Republic of Korea. The pool's honor roll preserves the names of those memorialized. The total effect of the memorial is astonishing. The combination of stone, statuary, and water truly fulfills the memorial's intent: "Our nation honors her sons and daughters who answered the call to defend a country they never knew and a people they never met."[47]

Oklahoma City National Memorial

On April 19,1995, the nation was shocked by the bombing of the Alfred P. Murrah Federal Building in Oklahoma City, Oklahoma. On April 19, 2000, the Oklahoma City National Memorial was dedicated. The memorial mission's statement is poignant and evocative: "We come here to remember those who were killed, those who survived and those changed forever. May all who leave here know the impact of violence. May this memorial offer comfort, strength, peace, hope and security."

After an international competition, the German-based Butzer Design Partnership was selected to design the memorial; its principal designers were Hans Butzer, Torrey Butzer, and Sven Berg.[48] The memorial stands on a three-acre site that includes remnants of the original building. The main elements of the outdoor section of the memorial include the Gates of Time, which frame 9:02 AM, the moment of destruction; the Reflecting Pool, whose gently flowing water is meant to soothe wounds; the Children's Area, displaying tiles painted by children in 1995, as well as chalkboards for children who visit; the Rescuers' Orchard, a grove of flowering trees surrounding the Survivor Tree; the Survivor Tree, a 70-year-old symbol of resilience; and the Memorial Fence, where visitors continue to leave mementos.[49]

Visitors enter the memorial through large gates. The first symbolizes the time of 9:01 AM, just before the bombing. It is here that visitors read the memorial's mission statement. Later, visitors will exit through a second large gate, this one symbolizing 9:03 AM, the moment after lives were changed forever.

Between the two gates are a 400-foot reflecting pool and 168 empty chairs, one for each of the people killed in the blast. To the north of the chairs stands the Survivor Tree, an American elm which withstood that blast. There is also a museum which offers visitors a ten-chapter story in exhibits and recordings. "Included in the center is the Institute for the Prevention of Terrorism, a public-policy research center devoted to the study of terrorism and political violence," the living legacy of the memorial.[50]

The 168 empty chairs represent each lost life, a reminder of the loss felt by family members and friends. Each chair bears the name of a person lost on that dreadful day. The chairs are in nine rows, representing the nine floors of the building. The chairs are arranged according to the floor on which those killed either worked or were visiting. The chairs are constructed of bronze and stone.

The glass base bears the name of a victim. The chairs are two sizes, the smaller represents the loss of an individual [younger] than 19 years of age. By day, the chairs seem to float above the sacred ground, by night the glass bases illuminate [like] beacons of hope.[51]

The ten chapters in the museum begin with "Chaos" and conclude with "Hope." Artifacts salvaged from the building are displayed; these include a clock, a pencil sharpener, a file cabinet, and other reminders of a day that started out like every other. Small cases in the center of the first room contained unclaimed possessions, keys, shoes, and the like. In the "Gallery of Honor," visitors can see images of each person killed in the bombing.

As visitors leave the final room, "Hope," they can see the outdoor memorial and pass by the "water wall," a "thin sheet of water flowing over a dark stone background, flanked on both sides by bronze wall. It provides continuity with the Outdoor Symbolic Memorial, which has a dark stone reflecting pool and bronze gates."[52]

Columbine Memorial

The goals of the team designing the memorial after the tragic shootings at Columbine High School, Littleton, Colorado, in 1999, included creating "a respectful place where family members, members of the community and visitors [could] come to gain an understanding of the innocent victims of Columbine." The committee also hoped to use materials native to the area and to incorporate the Columbine "never forgotten" ribbon into the design.[53]

A spot at the southeastern edge of Clement Park was chosen for the memorial. Rushing water is used to muffle the sounds of other park activities and help visitors enter into quiet, solitude, and meditation.

The interior of the memorial is an oval stone outer wall softened by a grove of trees in the center and low native plantings around the edges. Steep landforms of the existing hills gently fold back from the top of the outer retaining wall. These hills surround . . . the memorial, embracing, comforting and protecting the visitor and the community.[54]

The inner Ring of Remembrance, a low wall of stone, is actually a circle of stories: narrative remembrances from victims' families and friends are etched into the stone. The sound of water from the other side of the stone brings comfort as the visitor reads the reflections. The tails of an intricate ribbon design connects the Ring of Remembrance with the outer Ring of Healing, which is also etched with personal narratives. "Low groupings of native shrubs and flowers soften the stone and create an inviting garden environment. Benches are located in welcoming areas to all the visitors to sit in reflection and contemplation."[55]

Visitors leaving the site are led up one of two stone stairways. At the top of the stairways are small overlooks providing panoramic views of the Rocky Mountains and Columbine.

National World War II Memorial

Among the newest of American memorials, the National World War II Memorial, in its very design, pays tributes to America's "greatest generation."[56] "The memorial design creates a special place within the vast openness of the National Mall to commemorate the sacrifice and celebrate the vistory of WWII, yet remains respectful and sensitive to its historic surroundings."[57] The memorial lies between the Washington Monument at one end of the mall and the Lincoln Memorial at the other. Its location led one reporter to muse:

If the Washington Monument embodies our democratic ideals of the 18th century, and the Lincoln Memorial reflects their expansion in the 19th century, the World War II Memorial can be fairly said to represent the broadened view of democracy that was articulated in the 20th century. The conversation goes on unimpeded.[58]

The principal features of the memorial are the memorial plaza and the Rainbow Pool. Bases of granite and bronze are adorned with the emblems of the Army, Navy, Marine Corps, Army Air Forces, Coast Guard, and Merchant Marines. 24 bronze bas relief panels depict America's war years, both at home and overseas. Through these panels, based on war photographs, sculptor Raymond Kaskey tells the story of World War II, beginning with a family listening on their radio to the news of the bombing of Pearl Harbor, and ending with people receiving a peace-time delivery of Lend-Lease equipment.[59] Curved ramps provide entry into the plaza.[60]

"Two 43-foot arches serve as markers and entries on the north and south ends of the plaza. Bronze baldacchinos are an integral part of the arch design. Four bronze columns support four American eagles that hold a suspended victory laurel to memorialize the victory of the WWII generation."[61] A victory medal inlaid on the floor of the arches is surrounded by the inscriptions "1941-1945," "Victory on Land," "Victory at Sea," and "Victory in the Air."

Fifty-six granite pillars connected by a bronze rope celebrate the nation's unity during the war years. Each pillar, one for each state and territory of the era, as well as the District of Colombia, is adorned with oak and wheat bronze wreaths. A field of 4000 gold stars on the Freedom Wall commemorates the more than 400,000 Americans who gave their lives.[62]

The restoration of the Mall's Rainbow Pool served to provide a place where visitors may sit and reflect on the memorial while watching soothing waterfalls. The combination of landscaping and water gives the memorial the feel of gentle park. (Figure 2, page 21.) More than the Allied victory, the World War II memorial celebrates our coming together as a nation in a time of global crisis.

Garden of Stones

In September of 2003, Andy Goldsworthy's first permanent commission, *Garden of Stones*, opened in New York City. Although water is not a visible feature of this memorial, the design could not work without it. The Garden of Stones is an outdoor space at the Robert M. Morgenthau Wing of the Museum of Jewish History. It provides a quiet and beautiful place for visitors to honor the

12   *From the Rock Came Living Water*

memory of those who perished in the Holocaust and the sufferings of those who survived.

For *Garden of Stones*, Goldsworthy worked with nature's most elemental materials—stone, trees, and soil—to create a garden that is the artist's metaphor for the tenacity and fragility of life. Eighteen boulders form a series of narrow pathways in the Memorial Garden's 4,150-square-foot space. A single dwarf oak sapling emerges from the top of each boulder, growing straight from the stone. As the trees mature in the coming years, each will grow to become a part of the stone, its trunk widening and fusing to the base.[63]

Goldsworthy sees the garden as a symbol of the tension between "the un-yielding and the pliable;" in other words, through it, he celebrates the possibility of survival and growth in the midst of impossible conditions. The memorial also evokes the Jewish custom of placing stones on graves as a sign of remembrance. Goldsworthy hopes people will return to the garden at different seasons and throughout the years, experiencing it differently at each visit.[64]

Goldsworthy chose to include eighteen boulders in part because of the number's symbolic significance: In Hebrew every letter also possesses a number value. *Chai*, whose number value is 18, is the Hebrew word for life, and is know to many in the tradition toast "L'chaim"—to life![65]

Holocaust Memorial, Miami, Florida

The main part of Miami's memorial to the six million Jews who perished in the Holocaust is a 42-foot sculptured bronze arm. The arm, which soars upward, is surrounded by portrayals of victims helping victims; the memorial also includes a meditation garden. The architect and sculptor, Kenneth Treister, was commissioned to create a memorial which would "memorialize [the Holo-caust's] victims, serve as solace to its survivors, and also inform with factual representations in pictures and words of the 20th century's greatest human crime."[66]

The memorial is constructed of bright Jerusalem stone, combined with black granite lining the walls. The reflecting pool, 200 feet in diameter and filled with huge lily pads, reflects the memorial and offers visitors a place for quiet reflection.

The exhibits include a sculpture of a mother and two children as news of the Holocaust begins to leak out; a wooden arbor with white bougainvillea vines; a Dome of Contemplation, with a memorial flame and an inscription from the Twenty-Third Psalm; and a sculpture of an outstretched arm with a number from Auschwitz tattooed on it. The final sculpture, "Never Shall We Forget,"[67] is a reminder of the sculpture at Dachau in Germany, commissioned by survivors and carrying in three languages the inscription, "Never Again."

World Trade Center Memorial (1993)[68]

In 1993, a bomb exploded deep in the underground parking area between Tower One and Tower Two of the World Trade Center. The explosion killed six people and wounded many others. Elyn Zimmerman, the sculptor commissioned to create a memorial to this event, met with the families of those who had died before submitting a proposal. The memorial took the form of a circular fountain in red, black, and white granite.[69]

Zimmerman describes the fountain as "very modest." Water came out of small hole and flowed evenly over the sides of the disk. The red disk was inscribed with the names of the six who died in the bombing. Zimmerman purposely made the inscription small enough that people would have to walk up to the fountain to read it: "On February 26, 1993, a bomb set by terrorists exploded below this site. This horrible act of violence killed innocent people, injured thousands, and made victims of us all." The inscription was in both English and Spanish to honor the many victims of Hispanic origin.[70]

On September 11, 2001, Zimmerman, who lives near the World Trade Center site, saw the planes and watched the buildings collapse. The sculptor was hit by the realization that the fountain, which was now completely destroyed, represented a renewed loss for the families of those it commemorated.

World Trade Center Memorial (2001)

Following the second bombing of the World Trade Center, the World Trade Center Memorial Foundation, Inc. began to plan for a new memorial. The foundation's mission statement reflects the enormity of the task:

- Remember and honor the thousands of innocent men, women, and children murdered by terrorists in the horrific attacks of February 26, 1993 and September 11, 2001.
- Respect this place made sacred through tragic loss.
- Recognize the endurance of those who survived, the courage of those who risked their lives to save others, and the compassion of all who supported us in our darkest hours.
- May the lives remembered, the deeds recognized, and the spirit reawakened be eternal beacons, which reaffirm respect for life, strengthen our resolve to preserve freedom, and inspire an end to hatred, ignorance and intolerance.[71]

In 2004, after a long competition, a new design for the World Trade Center Memorial was unveiled. The design includes "a canopy of 60-foot oak trees, an exposed 70-foot-tall section of the ground zero slurry wall, and a curtain of falling water through which the victims' names will be visible"[72] The memorial commemorates the events of September 11, 2001, when the twin towers were destroyed and 2,749 people were killed.

The revised plan "preserves a majority of the sheared-off remnants of the tower footings that sit encased in concrete 70 feet below street level, including almost all of the North Tower footprint."[73] According to Michael Arad, architect, and Peter Walker, landscape architect, "This memorial [offers] a space that resonates with the feelings of loss and absence that were generated by the destruction of the World Trade Center and the taking of thousands of lives on September 11, 2001 and February 26, 1993."[74]

The memorial, titled "Reflecting Absence," for which ground was finally broken in March of 2006, encompasses the footprints of the two towers with a field of trees and two large voids containing recessed pools. Ramps lead down to underground memorial spaces.

Descending into the memorial, visitors are removed from the sights and sounds of the city and immersed in a cool darkness. As they proceed, the sound of water falling grows louder, and more daylight filters in from below.

At the bottom of their descent, they find themselves behind a thin curtain of water, staring out at an enormous pool. Surrounding this pool is a continuous ribbon of names. The enormity of this space and the multitude of names that form this endless ribbon underscore the vast scope of the destruction. Standing there at the water's edge, looking at a pool of water that is flowing away into an abyss, a visitor to the site can sense that what is beyond this curtain of water and ribbon of names is inaccessible.[75]

The designers, reflecting on the "haphazard brutality" of the events, decided not to arrange the names in any particular order, thus making "no attempt to impose order upon this suffering."[76] A directory will be available to guide visitors to particular names. Spaces have been set aside for quiet contemplation and for lighting candles or leaving small mementos. A very private room has been designed for unidentified remains. An underground interpretive center will contain preserved artifacts and personal effects, and provide space for lecture halls and a research library.[77]

Conclusion

And so it continues. Like our earliest ancestors, we today feel the need to commemorate loss and celebrate memory. And we turn to ancient symbols of endurance and change, symbols of stone and water, to help us grieve our loss and get on with the business of creating a better world. Designers of these memorials hope both to preserve sacred memories and to educate for the future. They provide us with quiet spaces to pause, to reflect, to weep, to express thanks. Their use of water and stone as vehicles of ritual memory enriches us all.

Notes

1. http://www.pbs.org/art21/artists/lin/card1.html. See also http://www.bluffton.edu/~sullivanm/Alabama;Montgomery/civilrts/lin.html; http://www.lectures.org/lin.html; http://pbs.org/pov1996mayalin_press.pdf; http://postcardsfrom.com/travt/travt-al.html; and http://www.roadtripusa.com/us_80/Alabama.html.

2. From James Weldon's Johnson's poem, "The Creation," in his collection of poetry, *God's Trombones: Seven Negro Sermons in Verse* (New York: Penguin Books, 1990), P. 20.

3. Virginia Hamilton, *In the Beginning: Creation Stories from Around the World* (San Diego, CA: Harcourt Brace Jovanovich, Publishers, 1988), pp. 133-135.

4. Richard Y. Hathorn, *Greek Mythology* (Beirut, Lebanon: American University of Beirut, 1977), pp. 14, 17-18. See also Thomas H. Carpenter and Robert J. Gula, *Mythology Greek and Roman* (Wellesley, MA: The Independent School Press, 1977), p. 70.

5. Carl-Martin Edsman, "Stones," David Mel Paul and Margareta Paul, trans. in Mircea Eliade, ed., *The Encyclopedia of Religion* (New York: Macmillan Publishing Company, 1987), p. 49

6. Udo Becker, *The Continuum Encyclopedia of Symbols*, Lance Larmer, trans. (New York: The Continuum Publishing Company, Inc., 1994), p. 283.

7. G. A. Gaskell, *Dictionary of Scripture and Myth* (New York: Dorset Press, 1988), p. 722.

8. Isaac Broyé, "Stone and Stone-Worship," in Isidore Singer, ed., *The Jewish Encyclopedia* Volume 11 (New York: KTAV Publishing House, Inc., no date given), p. 557.

9. Becker, p. 283. See also M. R. P. McGuire, "Stones, Sacred," in Berard L. Mathaler, ed., *New Catholic* Encyclopedia Volume 13 (Washington, DC: Catholic University of America Press, 2003), pp. 541-542. It is interesting to note that, in the case of violent death, the memorial marker was often erected on the spot where the victim was killed, a custom all too familiar in our own time.

10. Edsman, p. 50.

11. McGuire, p. 542. Sacred stones, or *massebot*, were also used during ceremonies of covenant ratification, such as that at Sinai (Ex. 24:4). Moses set up twelve of these stones to signify the acceptance of the covenant by the twelve tribes.

12. Ibid., pp. 50-51.

13. Gertrude Jobes, *Dictionary of Mythology, Folklore and Symbols Part 2* (New York: The Scarecrow Press, Inc., 1962), pp. 1495-1497.

14. J. E. Cirlot, *A Dictionary of Symbols Second Edition*, Jack Sage, trans. (New York: Dorset Press, 1971), pp. 313-314.

15. Gaskell, p. 723.

16. Jean Rudhardt, "Water," Erica Meltzer, trans., in Mircea Eliade, ed., *The Encyclopedia of Religion* (New York: Macmillan Publishing Company, 1987), p. 351.

17. Gaskell, p. 804.

18. Ibid., p. 807.

19. Becker, p. 322.

20. Cirlot, p. 364.

21. E. J. Gratsch, "Water, Liturgical Use of," in Marthaler, Volume 14, p. 660.

22. Rudhardt, pp. 354, 356.

23. Cirlot, p. 366.

24. Judah Eisenstein, "Water," in Isidore, p. 475.

25. Hirschel Revel, "Water," in Isaac Landman, ed., *The Universal Jewish Encyclopedia* Volume 10 (New York: KATV Publishing House, Inc., 1969), p. 475.

26. Gratsch, "Water," p. 660.

27. J.-P. Migne, ed., PG 32:188B [*Patrologiae cursus completes, Series graeca*] (Paris, 1857-66).

28. P. dePuniet, DACL [*Dictionnaire d'archéologie chrétienne et de liturgie*] 2:685f.

29. P. Magdalino, "Water," in Alexander Kazhdan, ed., *The Oxford Dictionary of Byzantium* (New York: Oxford University Press, 1991), p. 2191. See also, P. Magdalino, "The Literary Perception of Everyday Life in Byzantium," *Byzantinoslavica* 48 (1987), pp. 32ff.

30. Ibid.

31. Jobes., pp. 1667-1668.

32. Cirlot, p. 364.

33. Rudhardt, p. 357.

34. Eisenstein, p. 475.

35. Ibid., p. 476.

36. Rudhardt, p. 365.

37. Ibid.

38. Ibid., p. 366.

39. Louis Chochod, *Occultisme et magie en Extrême-Orient* (Paris, 1945), cited in Cirlot, p. 366.

40. "Stones and Mortar," http://www.nps.gov/nama/mortar/mortar.htm.

41. http://nps.gov/fdrm/memorial/memorial.htm.

42. http://www.exploredc.org/print.php?id=128&PHPSESSID=5405ffaflcc32cdeea d199bd2db9decc. It is interesting that the initial memorial made no reference to the polio that struck FDR as an adult, making it impossible for him to walk without assistance. After a campaign organized by the National Organization on Disability, an additional sculpture depicting FDR in his wheelchair was unveiled in 2000.

43. http://www.nps.gov/fdrm/home.htm.

44. http://www.nab.usace.arm.mil/projects/WashingtonDC/Korean.html.

45. Ibid.

46. Ibid.

47. Ibid. See also http://www.nps.gov/kowa. and http://www.nps.gove/ nama/ mortar/ mortar.htm.

48. http://www.okccvb.org/special/murrah.html.

49. http://www.nps.gov/okci/.

50. See note 48.

51. http://www.geocities.com/seanache2/okcity.htm.

52. http://www.oklahomacitynationalmemorial.org/memo_outd.htm.

53. http://www.columbinememorial.org/overview.html.

54. Ibid.

55. Ibid.

56. This is the generation honored by newsman Tom Brokaw in his book, *The Greatest Generation* (New York: Random House, 1998).

57. http://www.wwiimemorial.com.

58. Inga Saffron, "Monument to Democracy," *The Philadelphia Inquirer*, May 28, 2004, p. E5.

59. Ibid.

60. http://www.wwiimemorial.com.

61. Ibid.

62. Ibid. During the war, the gold star was given to families who lost someone to the war.

63. http://www.mjhnyc.org.

64. Ibid.

65. Ibid.

66. http://www.maintour.com.

67. Ibid.

68. In June, 2006, the memorial was redesigned. The names of the victims will be above-ground and the museum will be smaller, but the reflecting pools and waterfalls will be retained.

69. http://www.ifar.org/911_memorial1.htm.

70. Ibid.

71. http://en.wikipedia.org/wiki/World_Trade_Center_Memorial.

72. David M. Levitt, "A new plan for WTC memorial," *The Philadelphia Inquirer*, December 17, 2004, p. A10.

73. Ibid.

74. http"//www.wtcsitememorial.org.

75. Ibid.

76. Ibid.

77. Ibid.

Works Cited

Becker, Udo. *The Continuum Encyclopedia of Symbols*. Lance Larmer, trans. New York: The Continuum Publishing Company, Inc., 1994.

Brokaw, Tom. *The Greatest Generation*. New York: Random House, 1998.

Broyé, Isaac. "Stone and Stone-Worship." In Isidore Singer, ed. *The Jewish Encyclopedia*. Volume 11. New York: KTAV Publishing House, Inc. [no date given]

Carpenter, Thomas H. and Robert J. Gula. *Mythology Greek and Roman*. Wellesley, MA: The Independent School Press, 1977.

Chocod, Louis. *Occultisme et magie en Extrême-Orient* Paris, 1945.

Cirlot, J. E. *A Dictionary of Symbols. Second Edition*. Jack Sage, trans. New York: Dorset Press, 1971.

Edsman, Carl-Martin. "Stones." David Mel Paul and Margareta Paul, trans. in Mircea Eliade, ed. *The Encyclopedia of Religion*. New York: Macmillan Publishing Company, 1987.

Eisenstein, Judah. "Water." In In Isidore Singer, ed. *The Jewish Encyclopedia*. Volume 11. New York: KTAV Publishing House, Inc. [no date given]

Gaskell, G. A. *Dictionary of Scripture and Myth*. New York: Dorset Press, 1988.

Gratsch, E. J. "Water, Liturgical Use of." In Berard L. Mathaler, ed. *New Catholic Encyclopedia*. Volume 14. Washington, DC: Catholic University of America Press, 2003.

Hamilton, Virginia. *In the Beginning: Creation Stories from Around the World*. San Diego, CA: Harcourt Brace Jovanovich, Publishers, 1998.

Hathorn, Richard Y. *Greek Mythology*. Beirut, Lebanon: American University of Beirut, 1977.

http://en.wikipedia.org/wiki/World_Trade_Center_Memorial.

http://nps.gov/fdrm/memorial.htm.

http://nps.kowa.htm

http://nps.gov/nama/mortar/mortar.htm.

http://postcardsfrom.com/travt/travt-al.html.

http://www.bluffton.edu/~sullivanm/Alambama;Montgomery/civilrts/lin.html.

http://www.columbinememorial.org.
http://www.exploredc.org/print.php?id_128&PHPSESSID=540ffaflcc32deead199bd2db9 decc.

http:www.geocities.com/seanache2/okcity.htm.

http://www.ifar.org/911_memorial1.htm.

http://www.lectures.org/lin.html.

http://www.maintour.com

http://www.mjhny.org.

http://www.nabusace.arm.mil/projects.WashingtonDC/Korean.html.

http://www.oklahomacitynationalmemorial.org/memo_outd.htm.

http://www.okccvb.org/special/murrah.html.

http:www.pbs.org/art21/artists/lin/card1.html.

http://www.roadtripusa.com/us_80/Alabama.html.

http://www.wtcsitememorial.org.

http://www.wwiimemorial.com

Jobes, Gertrude. *Dictionary of Mythology, Folklore and Symbols. Part 2*. New York: The Scarecrow Press, Inc., 1962.

Johnson, James Weldon. *God's Trombones: Seven Negro Sermons in Verse*. New York: Penguin Books, 1990.

Levitt, David M. "A new plan for WTC memorial." *The Philadelphia Inquirer.* December 17, 2004. A10.

Magdalino, P. "The Literary Perception of Everyday Life in Byzantium." *Bzyantinoslavica* 48. 1987. 32ff.

_____. "Water." In Alexander Kazhdan, ed. *The Oxford Dictionary of Byzantium* New York: Oxford University Press, 1991.

McGuire, M. R. P. "Sontes, Sacred." In Berard L. Mathaler, ed. *New Catholic Encyclopedia.* Volume 13. Washington, DC: Catholic University of America Press, 2003.

Migne, J.-P., ed. PG 32:188B [*Patrologiae cursus completes. Series graeca*] Pris, 1957-66.

Puniet, P. de. DACL [*Dictionnaire d'archéologie chrétienne et de liturgie*] 2:685f.

Revell, Hirschel. "Water." In Isaac Landman, ed. *The Universal Jewish Encyclopedia.* Volume 10. New York: KATV Publishing House, Inc., 1969.

Rudhardt, Jean. "Water." Erica Meltzer, trans. in Mircea Eliade, ed., *The Encyclopedia of Religion.* New York: MacMillan Publishing Company, 1987.

Saffron, Inga. "Monument to Democracy." *The Philadelphia Inquirer.* Mary 28, 2004. E5.

Chapter Two

Light on Sacred Stones

Thérèse McGuire, SSJ

Introduction: The Aesthetic Concept of Light and Beauty
> The aesthetics of proportion always remained a quantitative aesthetics. It could never explain satisfactorily the medieval pleasure in light and color, which was a qualitative experience.[1]

Leonard Callahan defined aesthetics as, "The philosophical study of beauty itself and its application to art and nature."[2] In order to understand the importance of the concept of light and beauty embraced by centuries of scholars, this essay will include an investigation of the ancient aesthetic views, which became the building blocks of medieval aesthetic principles. These building blocks of aesthetic theories prompted Abbot Suger in the twelfth century to usher in a new concept of the beauty of light streaming through stained glass windows creating an atmosphere of heavenly light reflecting on the "sacred stones" of the walls of monastic churches and cathedrals.

During the height of the Roman Empire, a certain degree of connoisseurship in aesthetics had been achieved, but this expertise tended to be lost during the period following the confusion resulting from the barbarian invasions. Those who had access to ancient manuscripts found it necessary to rediscover earlier aesthetic tenets. Naturally, Christian scholars and writers assigned new uses, as well as new meanings, to the tenets of aesthetic thought that had been established in antiquity. Wladyslaw Tatarkiewicz stated that the writings of both Greek and Latin Patristic Fathers of the Christian Church, "contain so many statements on beauty and art that one can build a reasonably complete aesthetic from them."[3]

Benedetto Croce recognized that, "Almost all the developments of ancient Aesthetic were continued by tradition or reappeared by spontaneous generation in the course of the Middle Ages."[4] Some of the basic concepts of beauty and art expounded by medieval scholars were firmly rooted in the theories and sentiments expressed by earlier Patristic Scholars. Certain concepts, not universally accepted in ancient philosophy, had remained as isolated insights; individual medieval scholars embraced these concepts also. "Augustine's assimilation of Platonic thought emerged in the theories of the school of Chartres almost a thousand years later; Johannes Scotus Erigena (9th Century) espoused the theories of Plotonius (c. 203-270); Robert Grosseteste (1174-1253) adopted the theories of the Pythagoreans; and Aristotle's teachings found an echo in the works of the Angelic Doctor, St. Thomas Aquinas (1225-1274)."[5]

Although medieval philosophers had not yet initiated specific formulas for the discipline of aesthetics, there existed many specifically aesthetic comments and conceptual distinctions in their works: "When Basil extended the concept of aesthetic proportion to the relation of object to subject; or Augustine extended the concept of rhythm to the soul; when Erigena defined the aesthetic attitude as disinterested; and Hugh of St. Victor classified types of beauty and Vitelo its sources; when Bonaventure described the stages of aesthetic experience and Thomas Aquinas defined beauty, they were introducing strictly aesthetic ideas."[6]

The theory of emanation put forward by Plotonius and Pseudo-Dionysius was founded on the analogy of light. It was assumed that BEING (the Godhead) has the nature of light, and that absolute beauty in particular radiates like light, and that absolute beauty in particular radiates beauty in this way. Panofsky asserted, "In the Middle Ages and especially in twelfth century thought, goodness and beauty were associated with light."[7] Thus light entered as a fundamental concept into aesthetics. Light remained essentially one of the basic tenets of even ancient aesthetics.

Ananda Coomaraswamy proposes that Dionysius the Pseudo-Areopogite expounded the fundamental tenet of medieval aesthetic in the, "Brief Treatment of the Beautiful" as found in his work, *De Divinis Nominibus* (Concerning Divine Names). Bonaventure proposed, "Light is the most beautiful, the most pleasant and the best among physical things."[8] Grosseteste produced an implied aesthetics of light, which was scholastic in outlook: "The nature of light is such that its whole beauty is based not on number, not on measure, and not on weight or anything else like it, but on sight . . . light shows their beauty in the highest degree.[9] Aquinas toward the end of the Middle Ages summed up the aesthetic concepts of the whole period defining beauty and light more exactly and explaining that those objects are called beautiful which evoke the pleasure of direct seeing and contemplation. "Beauty . . . is the object of cognitive power, for we call beautiful, things which give pleasure when they are seen."[10]

Stones too played an important role in the evolution of humanity's efforts to express the necessity of submission to a Higher Power. The light of the sun, so often equated with divine powers, shared in this equation. When the two components were carefully combined, humanity discovered a way to worship Divinity. The transformation of the physical environment by human intervention can be traced back at least to the eighth or ninth millennium to the configuration of mammoth megalithic stones placed in mysterious patterns on multiple sections of the globe. The symbolism of these patterns has baffled scholars throughout the centuries. These incomprehensible messages from the past seem to have roared over the windswept plains for centuries seeking for understanding and recognition from each generation, but the subsequent generations did not hold the keys of interpretation.

There is little doubt in the minds of scholars that intelligent beings constructed these mysterious megalithic monuments. Gerald Hawkins, commenting on the "cleverness" of prehistoric people who had discovered the wheel, the plow, the inclined plane, the sailboat, the lever, the process of loom weaving, and so forth, considered: "they were not clumsy hulky Neanderthalish creatures more animal than human."[11] Pierre Teilhard de Chardin, the French philosopher and Jesuit priest, commenting on the cave paintings of Lascaux wrote, "organically speaking the faculties of our remote forebears were probably the equal of our own. By the middle of the last Ice Age, at the latest, human beings had attained to the expression of aesthetic powers calling for intelligence and sensibility developed to a point which we have not surpassed."[12]

The meanings of the precise patterns of these megaliths, and the methods of construction have baffled scholars since the time of recorded history. Modern scholars may never discern these meanings either, since the mute mysterious megaliths were constructed well before written history.

Roman ingenuity produced the arch and the dome. Domes represented the dome of the heavens, so Roman architects devised an oculus in the center of the dome to allow the light to stream into the temple at all hours of the day. With this devise they hoped to gratify not only the gods, but also to please any worshipers who visited the Pantheon, that timeless temple for all the gods in Rome.

During the Romanesque period, leaded colored glass allowed some light to penetrate the thick walls of basilicas and churches. Beautiful mosaics reflected lights from candles on the multicolored tesserae, as well as from alabaster windows in the cathedral of Ravenna which filtered sunlight onto richly decorated gold and colored tesserae. But, "only with Abbot Suger of Saint Denis (1081-1151) did the windows dissolve the walls of churches."[13] In the Middle Ages Abbot Suger, of the Abbey of St. Denis in Paris, ushered in a new concept of the beauty of light streaming through stained glass windows to create an atmosphere of heavenly light reflected on the "sacred stones" of the walls of abbey churches and cathedrals. Such beauty was to be regarded by the faithful as God's grace illuminating the soul with an extraordinary variety of colorful beauty. Thus were born those magnificent canticles in stone, the Gothic Cathedrals.

Stonehenge

> Art and religion are the two great mirrors of any civilization, and in the absence
> of any clear knowledge of them one is lost. Yet there broods over Neolithic
> Britain a slightly chilling aura of an intensely practical culture, far more con-
> cerned with expressing itself in massive feats of engineering than in any more
> personal way, as if what it truly wanted to impress was neither gods nor other
> men, but matter itself.[14]

Some thirty-five centuries have passed since the great stones of "The Giants' Dance" (an ancient name for Stonehenge) appeared on Salisbury Plains in
the county of Wiltshire, situated in the Wessex district of southern England.
Since then scholars, poets, scientists, and religious theorists have endeavored to
unlock the enigma that surrounds the mystery of these silent sentinels of stone.
Why did the oral history of Stonehenge not survive throughout the silent centuries that preceded the first recorded history? Why did ancient inhabitants of that
plain fail to continue to relate their oral traditions about them? Were the inhabitants of the Salisbury Plains so accustomed to the sight of these mysterious
megalithic stones that they held no interest for them and therefore they no longer
questioned the meaning of their existence? What a tremendous void their lack of
communication has engendered for modern scholars!

Who were the people who built Stonehenge? What message did they hope
to convey when they constructed and so carefully placed these megaliths?
Stonehenge is first and foremost a, "cultural monument; it cannot be taken out of
its time and place."[15] The time was almost four thousand years ago; the place
was Britain. The identities of these extraordinary stonemasons, who had the
strength and the knowledge to bring together and to build this powerful assemblage of gigantic rocks, which we know today as Stonehenge, will forever remain anonymous, as will the mysterious purpose of its existence. As Michael
Drayton in his poem, "Polyolbion," mused: "Ill did those mighty men to trust
thee with their story; that has forgot their names who reared thee for their
glory."[16]

Mysterious Stonehenge may be, but few can discountenance the effect of
this assemblage of strange silent stones upon those who come to stare and ponder. John Fowles shared his insight about the excitement he felt at the impact the
sight of these stones had upon him when he first encountered them: "Where the
wiser judge architecture by the way it plays with light and space, I tend to judge
it by what it shuts out of those things. Stonehenge's marvelous openness to them
[light and space] was what first pleased me. It came to me on that occasion, and
has remained since, as the most natural building, the most woven with light, sky
and space, in the world."[17]

"The name 'Stonehenge,' which is of Saxon origin (though the building is
very much older), comes from the roots of 'stone' and 'henge,' or hang.' It is the
place of hanging stones,' that is of the stone lintels of the sarsen circle and
horseshoe."[18] Chippindale describes the configuration of the placement of the
stones of the outer sarsen circle.[19] "Thirty squared uprights, of a variety of sand-

stone known as sarsen, are arranged in a true circle about one hundred feet in diameter. The five components of the building are, from the outside inwards: sarsen circle with continuous lintels, bluestone circle, sarsen horseshoe of trilithons, bluestone horseshoe, and altar stone."[20] The bluestones are distinctly bluish in color with pink specks in them and are untrimmed boulders. Originally there were perhaps sixty of them but today only six of them remain upright. Within the bluestone circle is the horseshoe of sarsen trilithons; each of the trilithons is an independent structure and the lintels are held together with mortise-and-tenon joints. Only three of the trilithons remain intact; "The surviving upright of the great trilithons, of which twenty-two feet are above ground and another eight feet below, is the tallest of the ancient stones still standing in the British Isles. All fifteen stones making up the trilithons are still there."[21] The altar stone is a single large slab of gray-green sandstone, which differs geologically from the sarsen stones. It derived the name altar stone from the weather-hollowed indentations on the surface of the slab resembling basins for holding blood from sacrifices. Weather conditions throughout the centuries have hollowed out these indentations in diverse places, which collect rainwater, leading to the supposition by some scholars of the eighteenth century that the altar stone was meant to collect the blood of victims of sacrifice. There exists no proof that victims were sacrificed here.

For the past nine hundred years numerous scholars have published articles about Stonehenge, but definitive conclusions as to its origin and meaning have been colored by private interpretations throughout those nine centuries. Fascination for those megalithic stones has fed the imagination of scholars of every age which in turn has led to varied and interesting speculations usually colored by whatever current beliefs existed in the scholar's own society. Horace Walpole commented, "It is remarkable that whoever has treated of this monument has bestowed on it whatever class of antiquity he was particularly fond of."[22] For example:

1. Geoffrey of Monmouth, twelfth century, England's first national historian, looked upon Stonehenge as a memorial for those war heroes who died in the name of post-Roman patriotism. He concluded that Merlin the Magician transported the stones from Ireland by magic and then set them in their mysterious ponderous patterns.
2. Indego Jones, seventeenth century surveyor general to the king who returned Italian architecture to Britain for the glory of the monarchy, saw in Stonehenge a Roman temple dedicated to imperial grandeur.
3. Walter Charleton, physician to Charles II, devised the theory that Stonehenge was the place that witnessed the crowning of Britain's early kings.
4. The antiquarians John Aubrey and William Stuckeley, products of the liberal philosophy engendered by the violence of the French revolution, saw in Stonehenge a temple of resurgent nativism directed by British Druids against Roman conquest.
5. Gerald Hawkins, a twentieth/twenty-first century astronomer at the Smithsonian Astrophysical Observatory in Cambridge, Massachusetts, finds in

Stonehenge a scientific observatory for the prediction of solar and lunar events. He explains his theory: "We build electronic computers, so the ancients must have built rude prototypes anticipating our own concern with science and technology."[23]

The meaning of Stonehenge lies buried with its builders in the Salisbury Plains, which surround it. For the foreseeable future, it will remain cloaked in the mists that sometimes enshroud that mysterious plain. The poet Siegfried Sassoon attempted to express this mystery:

> What is Stonehenge? It is the roofless past;
> Man's ruinous myth; his uninterred adoring
> Of the unknown in sunrise cold and red; . . .
> The stones remain; their stillness can outlast
> The skies of history hurrying overhead. [24]

Throughout thirty-five centuries, rays of light from the sun, the moon and the stars have illumined the silent stones that configure the monument of Stonehenge, but modern scholars are no closer to solving the mystery of its "why or wherefore." Whether or not these stones were considered sacred from the time that their patterns were positioned on the Salisbury Plain will remain a mystery for scholars after us to ponder. Perhaps John Fowles said it best, "Though we can't read it in words, a first declaration was made: man grew ambitious, and impatient with his ephemerality. Stonehenge is not simply a memorial to its Bronze Age builders; it is a memorial to a dream, and a dream still dreamt by each. Something of me shall survive."[25]

Centuries have passed but the questions remain unanswered. Why is the modern world so fascinated with these megaliths? How many secrets lie beneath the light as it casts its rays on these silent, stationary sentinels of stone? Gerald Hawkins concluded: "The names of the mighty men, and perhaps women, who built Stonehenge may indeed be forever forgotten, but their story is still being read, and interpreted, and more and more remembered in the stones today."[26] Henry James sums up his experience on visiting Stonehenge:

> You may put a hundred questions to these rough-hewn giants as they bend in grim contemplation of their fallen companions; but your curiosity falls dead in the vast sunny stillness that enshrouds them, and the strange monument, with all its unspoken memories, becomes simply a heart stirring picture in a land of pictures. . . . There is something in Stonehenge almost reassuring; and if you are disposed to feel that life is rather a superficial matter . . . the immemorial gray pillars may serve to remind you of the enormous background of time.[27]

Stonehenge contains the secrets of a dead society that can never speak to us directly but can offer up only mute testimony to the archaeologist or at best pass the faintest whispers through the epic literature of its descendants. But the presence of sacred stones dedicated to specific deities appeared after history began to be recorded. The Old Testament records several such stones.

Biblical Stones

> When as Genesis relates, God praised the beauty of the world and declared it good, this was not because the world was pleasing to his senses, but because it had fulfilled the purpose for which it was created. St. Basil of Caesarea (329-379)

Centuries after the mysterious megalithic stone configurations settled on the Salisbury Plains, scholars discovered a method of recording the deeds and beliefs of contemporary generations. Baked clay, papyrus, linen, vellum, and parchment all served to record human exploits. Humanity's discovery of God and of God's revelations to humankind found expression in the written word. Hebrew scholars delighted in discussing and recording God's love for humanity, especially for the Chosen People. The earliest accounts of the Hebrew's quest for knowledge of the creation of the world and humanity's place in it resulted in the Book of Genesis, the first Book of the Bible.[28]

The Old Testament records numerous accounts of Biblical personages who regarded stones as sacred and utilized such stones as memorials to Yahweh's special relationship with them. From the earliest book of the Bible, Genesis 34:1-4, we have the account of Jacob (Israel). When Jacob and his family lived in the country of the Canaanites, his daughter fell under the spell of Shechem, a Canaanite, who raped her but then fell in love with her. He wished to marry her so he approached her family for permission. He was told that he might have her as his wife if he and all the young men in Canaan would submit to circumcision, which they did. Her brothers attacked the young men, who were still suffering from the rite of circumcision; all the Canaanite men were slaughtered in retaliation for the defilement of their sister. Jacob feared for the safety of his family so he fled with them from that place to Lutz. Jacob built an altar there to honor Yahweh for the safe deliverance for his family. That night Yahweh appeared to Jacob in a dream and said to him, "I am El Shaddai . . . I give you this land . . . and I will give this land to your descendants after you." Jacob raised a monument in the place where he had spoken with El Shaddai, a stone monument on which he made a libation and poured oil. Jacob named the place Bethel, the place where God had spoken to him." Genesis, 35: 1.

After the Exodus from Egypt, when Yahweh had delivered his people from the hands of Pharaoh, the people wandered in the desert under many trying circumstances. Yahweh wished to share with them the way of life which would bring them peace, happiness and joy, so he spoke with Moses on the mountain and then wrote with his own finger the laws of the covenant on two tablets of stone. As the Book of Exodus explains: "When he had finished speaking with Moses on Mount Sinai, Yahweh gave him two tablets of the Testimony, tablets of stone inscribed by the finger of God." (Exodus 31:18)

Years later, when Joshua was far advanced in years, he summoned the people to remind them of all that Yahweh had done for them and to exhort them to remain faithful to Yahweh and to His commandments even in the midst of the unbelievers where they lived. Joshua gathered all the people together at Shechem. Some of the people of Israel had begun to worship false gods in the land of Shechem and Joshua warned them of the consequences they would suffer for deserting Yahweh. He reminded them of all that Yahweh had done for them while they were still God's people and he made them choose the path they would follow. "So now put away the gods that your ancestors served beyond the River and in Egypt, and serve Yahweh." He told the people that he and his household would remain faithful to El Shaddai. The people answered that they too would remain faithful to Yahweh. "We too will serve Yahweh, for he is our God." On that day, Joshua made a covenant for the people; He laid down a statute and ordinance for them at Shechem. Joshua wrote these words in the Book of the Law of God. Then he took a great stone and set it up there under the oak tree in the sanctuary of Yahweh, and Joshua said to the people, 'See! This stone shall be a witness against us because it has heard all the words that Yahweh has spoken to us: it shall be a witness against you in case you deny your God.' Then Joshua sent the people away, each to his own inheritance. (Joshua 24: 25-28)

Many other times the people of the Old Testament demonstrated their reverence for Yahweh by building altars of stone or by selecting one special stone to anoint and set aside for the worship of Yahweh. But people from other regions such as the Egyptians, the Greeks and the Romans, discovered that there had to be a sublime deity who ruled over them and required acts of worship from them. These people also endeavored to worship their gods and often resorted to erecting the finest buildings in which to worship them. Thus were born the architectural wonders of the Greek and Roman temples to honor their gods. Many times these temples were erected on the highest land in their cities so that they might be seen from great distances.

The Pantheon

The ambition and daring of the Pantheon design are utterly Roman, but in its planetary rotundity the building is also suffused with a quality of seeking for the comprehension of things beyond knowledge, a quality that records Roman sensitivity to human limits. The Pantheon exists because of a particular man, but the stirring and eloquent message preserved in the universality of its forms belongs to everyone. This is why it is the temple of the whole world.[29]

Agrippa, the minister of Augustus, built and dedicated the original Pantheon in 25 BCE; it consisted of a rectilinear, T-shaped structure with masonry walls and a timber roof. It burned in the great fire of 80 CE. Emperor Domitian rebuilt it, but the second one, erected on the same site, was destroyed when lightning struck it in 110 CE. Both buildings were destroyed before Hadrian's accession to the throne. Hadrian had the building entirely replaced with the present structure in the Campus Maurius.[30] Rather than placing an inscription declaring his own endeavor in rebuilding the edifice, Hadrian restored Agrippa's original inscription on this new edifice. M. AGRIPPA. L. F. COSTERTIUM. FECIT (Marcus Agrippa the Son of Lucius, Three Time Consul, Built This) [31]

This inscription caused much confusion during the ensuing centuries. Since the present Pantheon was constructed of poured concrete and then faced with brick, definite proof about the time of the present building's construction can be found in the brick stamps that identify each brick as to the time of its manufacture. These stamps pressed into the soft bricks before firing are of enormous help in identifying the time of the building's construction. According to the stamps on the bricks, the building was begun around July of 118 AD and was finished between the years 125 and 128 AD. They prove conclusively that the entire edifice dates from Hadrian's reign. "The Pantheon was part of Hadrian's plan to mark the beginning and to proclaim the nature of the age that was to be his." [32]

Publius Aelos Hadrianus (76-138 CE) was born in Roman Spain during the reign of the emperor Vespasian. In his youth he served in the military as well as in various other government posts. Hadrian became a ward of his cousin the emperor Trajan in 85 CE, and his adopted son in 117 CE, thus establishing his right to the throne of Rome. Although Hadrian exhibited many flaws of character in his treatment of both Jews and Christians, he had the redeeming characteristics of a highly cultivated man, which added to his prestige as an emperor. He was, "conscientious, enlightened, romantic and a devotee of Greco-Oriental cults." [33]

In order to imply an imperial concern for all lands and peoples Hadrian began an extensive building program. In almost every city within the empire Hadrian erected public buildings, but his name appears only on the temple built in honor of his adopted father, Trajan. In order to mark the beginning of his building plan and to proclaim the nature of the age which was to be his, Hadrian rebuilt the Pantheon on the burnt ruins of the previous buildings.

Hadrian's Pantheon resembled a Greek temple but was far more elaborate. His plans called for a circular domed rotunda whose internal geometry would create a perfect sphere. The height of the rotunda to the top of its dome would match its diameter. The plans also called for a circular opening in the dome, which would be the only source of light. Hadrian explained:

> My intentions had been that this sanctuary of all gods should reproduce the likeness of the terrestrial globe and of the stellar sphere. The cupola . . . revealed the sky through the great hole in the center, showing alternately dark and blue. This temple, both open and mysteriously closed, was conceived as a solar quadrant. The hours would make their round on that caissoned ceiling so carefully polished by Greek artisans; the disk of daylight would rest suspended there like a shield of gold; rain would form in a clear pool on the pavement below, prayers would rise like smoke toward that void where we place the gods. [34]

The name Pantheon gives us the clue as to the purpose of the edifice; it was a *temlpum deorum omnium* (a temple for all the gods) constructed to honor all the gods, but Hadrian also envisioned it as a temple to the Roman universe. MacDonald explains: "Order, peace, unity –these were the immediate meanings of the Pantheon, cast in a religious setting. And it was a kind of orrery [35]as well, in which planetary implications were signaled directly as the earth revolved. Zeus-Jupiter-Helios, the supreme god allied with the Great Sun, was himself inside the rotunda, his effulgence visible but intangible."[36]

The sun, said the ancients, is the eye of Zeus, and in Hadrian's Pantheon the greatest of the gods was epiphanized in light. Above all it is the garment of light worn by the rotunda, which connects the individual with the heavens, and which appearing in movement on the architecture bridges the intangible with the tangible. "The long cylinder of light that is shaped by the oculus and pries through the building is one of the triumphs in architecture of the expression of a world feeling, a triumph that belongs to Hadrian."[37] The source of that magnificent ray of light is of course the sunlight pouring through the tremendous circular opening in the dome, the oculus. Both pagan and Christian worlds of thought considered domes as architectural symbols for the dome of heaven. Many of these domes contained an oculus, which symbolized a supposed opening in the sky, which would facilitate the sending and receiving of messages to and from the gods. Dio Cassius theorizes that the dome of heaven inspired the name Pantheon: "It is called thus possibly because it included images of many gods in its statues, amongst them those of Ares and of Aphrodite; but I believe that the reason is the similarity of its cupola-form to the heavens."[38]

One of the most compelling features of the dome of the Pantheon is its great oculus (eye of heaven), which opens the dome to the heavens and to a great shaft of light. This shaft of light provides the only source of light in the building itself. Grosseteste commenting on the function of light stated that, "Light is the beauty and the adornment of visible creation."

High up on the back wall of the porch of the Pantheon, there is an inscription placed there in 1632 by Urban VIII. The first three lines read: PANTHEON AEDIFICIUM TOTO TERRARUM ORBE CELEBERRIMUM (The Pantheon, the most celebrated edifice in the whole world.) One man's dream coupled with the Roman penchant for planning buildings, whose full visual impact occurs only at the right moment when the senses are ready, produced the Pantheon. "The Pantheon exists because of a particular man, but the stirring and eloquent message preserved in the universality of its forms belongs to everyone. That is why it is the temple of the whole world."[39]

The Pantheon was made for light. It captures light and even conquers it, and natural light is not a static thing. It was the prize for which all this concrete was poured. The architect shaped his building to form and manipulate a great shaft of illumination, a visible, almost tangible rod of solar effusion. Everything in the building is subordinated to it. As the earth rotates, Hadrian's sun-show spins on.[40]

Almost as spectacular as the great shaft of light that streamed through the oculus was another form of stone that shimmered with reflected light—the colorful mosaics brought to Italy from Byzantium.

Ravenna

> Ravenna artists knew, as Seurat and the Pointillists were to discover a millennium and a half later, that fragments of pure color, seen at a proper distance, can coalesce into Images of density and power.[41]

In view of the fact that Mosaic Law forbade the use of images of God in art, scholars have not been able to confirm with certainty the reasons why the early Christians, after the Roman persecutions ended, decided to decorate their places of worship with images of God and of the saints. The influence of ancient Roman murals and mosaics certainly must have played an important role. Greco-Roman artists utilized mosaic stones on their floors (only rarely on their walls) to depict their frolicking gods and goddesses; they adorned their walls with fresco paintings. Inheriting the technical virtuosity of centuries of Greco-Roman masters, Ravenna artists knew how to use the three hundred different shades of colored glass at their disposal. When Christian artists began to work with religious themes for their mosaics, they frowned upon using their religious subjects on floors for people to walk upon; rather they placed them on walls for the edification of all. What "we do know is that wall painting, principally in the form of mosaics soon became a standard feature of elaborate Christian churches, and that these visual programs were used not to educate the illiterate but to elucidate Christian theology or occasionally to teach moral lessons."[42]

Some of the most beautiful and well-known mosaics outside of Rome are those found in Ravenna, Italy, known as the town of mosaics of great beauty. Charles Sherrill hails Ravenna as "one of the four most important centers for mosaics."[43] The skill with which the artisans created these unusually beautiful mosaics rests mostly in the artistic use of the colors of the tesserae, a skill that has never been surpassed. Typically, mosaicists use thousands of pieces of *tesserae* (small pieces of colored glass enamels, fragments of gold sandwiched between pieces of glass, stones, chips of marble, and/or of mother-of-pearl) to create their masterpieces. Because of the nature of the material used, mosaics can and have survived for centuries without losing their shimmering colors. Sporadically some of the tesserae are tilted to catch the light at an angle causing them to create a shimmering illusion since, "when the light strikes them it is not reflected in a continuous beam as in a mirror but is refracted and broken up prismatically into as many chromatic units as there are tiny cubes of mosaic."[44]

In Ravenna the mosaics are bathed in the soft luminescence created by the sun shining through the alabaster windows during the day and by the flickering of candles after nightfall. The mosaicists spread the most graceful colors and the most delicate shades in the apses, cupolas, along the aisles, and on the arches of the church buildings. A palpable rhythm seems to flow around these representations where the Hellenistic-Roman and Byzantine architectural styles and decorations blend together.

Established as a seaport by Augustus, Ravenna provided an important naval base for the Roman fleet in the Eastern Mediterranean. When Augustus assigned the fleet to be stationed there for the defense of the Adriatic Sea, he ordered the port to be united to a town by a coastal road and an imperial suburb to be built. The strategic position of Ravenna near the marshes and surrounded with walls established its historical importance. In time, after Rome fell to the barbarians, Ravenna became the Capital of the Western Empire (403-476) governed by Honorius and Galla Placidia. The mausoleum of Galla Placidia remains the earliest of the ornate buildings. Built by Galla Placidia in the first half of the fifth century to be her final resting place, the building is in the form of a Latin cross. Although the lower half of the walls is covered in marble, the ceiling and the archways glow with gorgeous blue, gold and colored tesserae in all their classical beauty. Representing victory of life over death, the mosaic decorations were, "visualized sermons rather than visualized scriptures."[45]

The Basilica of St. Vitale, erected by Giuliano Argentario and consecrated by Archbishop Massimiano in 548 CE, is one of the most beautiful buildings in Ravenna. Even though many sidewalls outside the sanctuary remain unadorned plain bricks, the beauty and quality of the mosaics on the sanctuary walls remains consciously dramatic. The mosaic portraits of the Emperor Justinian I and his consort, the Empress Theodora, are included on the side walls of the nave. "The mosaics were not intended as mere wall decorations; they were an integral part of the architectural effect, enclosing the congregation in an atmosphere that was at once instructive and exciting."[46]

Karl Rahner, that eminent twentieth-century theologian, "is convinced that, what we see in our physical world discloses the mysterious presence of God. The material world is a window into the divine world, a place through which God can shine His own warmth and love."[47] And so we come to Abbot Suger who ushered in the Gothic Era and the stained glass windows where rays of glorious light dissolved the walls of lofty cathedrals as well as those of humble churches.

Medieval Stones

> The nature of light is such that its whole beauty is based not on number, not on measure, and not on weight or anything like it, but on sight . . . light makes things beautiful and shows their beauty in the highest degree.[48]

"The nature of art and the why and wherefore of artistic activity"[49] assume different perspectives at different ages in history and are reflected in the works of the creative geniuses of each era. Erwin Panofsky stated that in the Middle Ages, "and especially in twelfth century thought, goodness and beauty were associated with light." [50] This section will include an investigation of the aesthetic principles of the Middle Ages, which led up to and encouraged the advancement of the beautiful stained glass windows of the Gothic cathedrals of

Europe, of the British Isles, and eventually of the cathedrals, churches and other buildings of twentieth century North America.

Medieval scholars considered as the final authority for their concepts, the words of the Bible and the teachings of the Church Fathers.[51] Benedetto Croce recognized that, "Almost all the developments of ancient Aesthetic were continued by tradition or reappeared by spontaneous generation in the course of the Middle Ages."[52] Grosseteste, commentating on the use of light in the Bible, quoted the passage from the Old Testament, "Arise, shine; for your light has come, and the glory of the Lord has risen upon you.

For darkness shall cover the earth, and thick darkness the peoples; but the Lord will arise upon you, and his glory will appear over you. Nations shall come to your light, and kings to the brightness of your dawn!" Isaiah 60: 1-3: "In an age that many scholars formerly referred to as the *Dark Ages,* the presence of light assumed great importance since it was equated with beauty, thus light entered as a fundamental concept into aesthetics."[53] Church buildings reflected the medieval scholars' search for a means of depicting the beauty of heaven. Frederick Heer points out the symbolic use of space which medieval minds invested with a mystical quality.[54] Space, stone, and immensity were all attributions of holiness; the superimposition of towers and the presence of columns raised them to a still higher power. That which was holy and divine could be contained in a closed space; thus "masculine" walls of stone God, created this "feminine" space which housed the very presence of God. Stained glass windows filtered the light from the sun and bathed the stones with beautiful color just as the light of God's grace inundated the soul with celestial light and beauty. Indeed, theological attitudes toward the very material of the glass assumed symbolic proportions. Scholars concluded that glass was almost a, "mystical substance through which the light of God passed in order to illuminate the interior of the church [as well as the minds of the worshippers]. This Platonic function remained a belief until the end of the Middle Ages."[55] Stained glass filtered the light of God's grace in glorious colors; sculpture and painting told stories of Yahweh's special care and concern for all people, and sometimes of God's unfailing justice.

Since the symbolic use of stained glass constitutes the soul of Gothic art, one might validly turn to the parent monument of all Gothic Cathedrals, [56] the Abbey Church of Saint-Denis. Michael Cothren points out, "Stained glass has not always been the preferred pictorial medium of Christian places of worship. Opaque wall paintings in fresco or mosaic were much more common before the late twelfth century. Had it not been for one visionary abbot, situated in an extraordinarily wealthy monastery at a singularly important moment in history, another artistic medium might have received the attention of Christian patrons and worshipers."[57]

In the twelfth century Abbott Suger emerged as the champion of the aestheticians who promulgated the concept of grandiose art. Churchman, statesman, and patron of the arts, he rose from the very humble status of peasant to that of the most powerful man in France during the twelfth century. As Abbot of St. Denis, he was able to set in motion his aspirations for building and adorning the

House of God. He began the architectural plans for embellishing the Abbey Church of St. Denis, with the premise that the church building should be a fore-taste of heaven for the people. His exuberance for all things beautiful that might enhance the sanctuary of the Most High found expression in his own words: "I delighted in the beauty of the house of God, and the diverse color and shapeli-ness of the gems [which embellished the golden chalices and when suffused with light] detached me from my outward cares, and bearing me from material to the non-material sphere, inclined me to reflect on the diversity of holy virtues. It seemed to me then that I was in some wondrous region placed neither in the mere earth nor in the purity of heaven, and that by the grace of God, I could in like manner, be transferred from the lower to the higher world." [58]

Abbot Suger embraced Grosseteste's theory that, "Light is the beauty and the adornment of visible creation."[59] With this theory, Suger ushered in a new aesthetic concept of the beauty of light streaming through stained glass windows to create an atmosphere of heavenly light reflected on the "sacred stones" of the walls of his abbey church of St. Denis. Such beauty was to be regarded by the faithful as God's grace illuminating the soul with an extraordinary array of beauty symbolized by the wondrous variety of colors reflected on the stone walls. In the Middle Ages and especially in twelfth-century thought, goodness and beauty were associated with light.[60] Suger himself wrote, "The church shines with its middle part brightened. For bright is that which is brightly cou-pled with the bright. And bright is the noble edifice which is pervaded by the new light."[61]

Delighting in beautiful things that not only pleased God but also the senses of the people, Suger worked tirelessly to produce the most magnificent structure capable to any architect. Thus, some scholars believe, was born the Gothic ca-thedral. Panofsky said of Suger, "In a century unusually productive of saints and heroes, Suger excelled by being human." [62]

Scholars of the past assumed that the art of the Middle Ages was didactic. For many years, scholars believed that everything that it was deemed necessary for people to know about religion, the saints, the virtues and vices, and even the sciences, were all taught to the people by means of the stained glass windows, the wall paintings, and the statues around the doorways. They surmised that the *sancta plebs Dei* (the holy people of God) learned all they needed to know by looking at these wonders. A careful study of the complex linking of theology and scriptural texts with sometimes incomprehensible medieval symbolism leads modern scholars to surmise that only the educated monks, nuns and theologians truly understood the messages put forth by these windows. Even so, Meyer Schapiro believed that, "Through the medium of art the highest conceptions of the theologians and scholars penetrated to some extent the minds of even the humblest of the people."[63]

Inspired by the biblical scholarship of Rupert of Deutz (c 1075-1129/30), Suger chose the themes for all the windows.[64] Since these themes, and indeed the very designs of the windows of Saint-Denis, were imitated in other cathedrals of France, of England, and of Germany, the splendid twelfth century school of stained glass deserved to be called, "the School of Saint-Denis."[65]

The theory of Pseudo-Dionysius constituted a compromise between the Platonic notion of proportion and the Neo-Platonic notion of light: "It is not possible for our mind to reproduce without material things and to contemplate the heavenly hierarchies other than by using material means. For the thinking [person], phenomenal beauties become images of invisible beauty. Sensual fragrances are reflections of an intellectual cause, and material lights are images of the non-material source of brilliance."[66]

The theory that the intersection of light and art aided monastic devotion inspired Suger. His own words record his personal devotional experience in the church building:

> When out of my delight in the beauty of the house of God—the loveliness of the many colored stones has called me away from external cares, and worthy meditation has induced me to reflect, transferring that which is material from that which is immaterial, on the diversity of the sacred virtues: then it seems to me that I see myself dwelling as it were, in some strange region of the universe which neither exists entirely in the slime of the earth nor entirely in the purity of Heaven; and that by the grace of God, I can be transported from this inferior to that higher world in an anagogical[67] manner. [68]

The Church Fathers of the Second Vatican Council, in an effort to give universal directives for adorning and beautifying churches as well as to present guidelines for church architecture emphasized the fact that the Church does not designate any particular style of art as her own. Rather it has admitted styles from every era and from all nationalities according to the talents and circumstances of the people and the needs of the various rites of the different sects.

Contemporary Stones

> A visual work of art cannot tell its own story unaided. It yields up its message only to persistent inquiry that draws upon all the resources of cultural history, from religion to economics. And this is no less true of the remote past than of the twentieth century.[69]

Contemporary Stones: Basilica of the Assumption, Baltimore, Maryland

"The first place in the English speaking world that had religious freedom by law was Maryland," alleged Cardinal Keeler, referring to the Maryland Charter under which the English colony was inaugurated in 1634, as well as to the Toleration Act of 1639 adopted by the Colony's Assembly.[70] Throughout long and often unjust historical events, Maryland lost its distinct reputation as the religiously tolerant state, but it retained its claim as the seat of the nation's first Roman Catholic See and the first Roman Catholic cathedral. The Basilica of the Assumption in Baltimore enjoys a distinction second to none as a result of its prestigious heritage as the birthplace of America's oldest cathedral; it celebrated its two-hundredth birthday in 2006. "When ground was broken for the cathedral in 1806, Bishop John Carroll of Baltimore was the only Catholic bishop for the entire country, an area covering what is now thirty states."[71] In 1937, Pope Pius XI designated the cathedral a basilica; in 1993 it was acknowledged as a national shrine.

Interest in restoring this celebrated landmark caught the imagination of various historic minded groups who adopted the motto, "Restore the Light," for its fund-raising drive, thus renovation began to restore to its original state this masterpiece of neoclassical architecture envisioned and designed by Henry Latrobe.

Latrobe envisioned a building flooded with natural light filtering into the interior through clear glass windows as well as through the twenty-four massive skylights encircling the outer dome. The inner dome, sixty-five feet in diameter, has a twenty-two foot opening called an oculus (eye) at the top reminiscent of the dome of the Pantheon in Rome. In addition to the oculus, Latrobe envisioned twenty-four skylights surrounding the dome as well as clear glass windows in the walls of the nave that would flood the building with natural light filtering into the interior. "Restore the Light," the motto adopted for the fund-raising drive to restore the original cathedral, encouraged the planners to begin by restoring the twenty-four skylights in the church's outer dome, which originally flooded the interior with natural light. The skylights, of necessity, had to be painted over during the World War II blackouts. The architect Henry Latrobe referred to these massive skylights as "lumiere mysterieuse" or mysterious light. Unlike the Abbey Church of St. Denis, the light here does not stream through stained glass windows coloring the stone walls, but will once again stream onto the painted walls from clear glass windows which replicates Latrobe's original plan.

Thus we pass once more from the filtered light through glass shining onto sacred stones to light streaming onto a sacred solid solitary megalithic stone.

Contemporary Stones: Meditation Room at the United Nations

This house, dedicated to work and debate in the service of peace, should have a room dedicated to silence in the outward sense and stillness in the inner sense.[72]

The United Nations buildings stand on land donated by the United States of America, but the land holds the distinction of being an independent country devoted to the welfare of all nations. Dag Hammarskjold, as Secretary General of the United Nations, insisted that a room be set aside where delegates to the United Nations might be able to retire in the midst of weighty deliberations concerning the problems affecting all the peoples of the world, to meditate and to ponder their responses in silence. Therefore the members set aside a small area away from the noise, bustle, and hectic pace of the business of the day. This small meditation room provided a place where persons of all beliefs might find a restful silence. As a centerpiece for the room, the designers chose a great slab of raw iron ore, millions of years old, in its purest form to symbolize the qualities of timelessness and strength. The four-foot-high, oblong-shaped solitary slab, given to the United Nations as a gift from Sweden, weighs six tons. A single shaft of light strikes the solitary megalithic stone in a room of utter simplicity. No other symbol invades the sacred space.

This meditation room was first opened at Headquarters in October 1952. It is open for private meditation from 8 AM until 4:45 PM, Monday through Friday, except on holidays. It was designed to give members of the United Nations, as well as visitors to the building, a place to withdraw from the problems of the world in order to get in touch with their inner feelings. For those involved in solving the mammoth problems of the world, it provides a haven in which to contemplate their decisions for the welfare of humanity.

Painted by the Swedish artist, Bo Bresco, a fresco, nine feet by six and one-half feet adorns one wall. It consists of blue, white, gray and yellow geometric forms with the light pure colors intersecting to form deeper colors. It provides a non-intrusive, fitting background for the great slab of raw iron ore, which occupies the center of the room.

> But the stone in the middle of the room has more to tell us. We may see it as an altar empty, not because there is no God, not because it is an altar to an unknown god; but because it is dedicated to the God whom [humanity] worships under many names and in many forms. This stone in the middle of the room reminds us also of the firm and permanent in a world of movement and change. The block of iron ore has the weight and solidity of the everlasting. It is a reminder of that cornerstone of endurance and faith on which all human endeavors must be based. The material of the stone leads our thoughts to the necessity for choice between destruction and construction, [as well as] between war and peace. . . . The shaft of light strikes the stone in a room of utter simplicity. There is an ancient saying that the sense of a vessel is not in its shell, but in its void. It is for those who come here to fill the void with what they find in their center of stillness. Dag Hammarskjold, 1957.[73]

After Hammarskjold's tragic death in a plane crash while on a peace-keeping mission to Africa, the members of the General Council chose Barbara Hepworth's sculpture as a fitting memorial to that great man. The sculpture consists of a hugh stone slab pierced by a hole, which allows light to penetrate from both sides. Perhaps it provides a fitting symbol for the United Nations members, and for all people, that they must have the ability to see both sides of a problem, in addition to having the insight to understand the people of the world from different angles. Whatever the symbolism, the impressive stone monument stands as did so many ancient stones and monuments throughout the ages as a reminder that, "Art should be an experience that reminds people of the presence of God."[74]

Conclusion

Sacred stones, whether isolated in solemn grandeur, grouped together in mute companionship, opened to the ravages of time and weather, or protected by encompassing sturdy walls have inspired human beings throughout the centuries. Their massive proportions and seemingly eternal presence against the ravages of time and the elements have influenced humanity's longing for permanence in an impermanent world. When combined with the beauty of light shining upon them, sacred stones have aroused longings for beauty in the souls of artists and artisans alike. From pre-historic days, throughout Biblical and Classical cultures, into medieval times whose patrons of art valued light as the perfect form of beauty, and into our present era, light on sacred stones has motivated and encouraged cultural, aesthetic, and artistic heights of glory in human souls.

Notes

1. Umberto Eco, *Art and Beauty in the Middle Ages*, trans. Hugh Bredin, New Haven: Yale University Press, 1986, 42.

2. Leonard Callahan, O.P., *A Theory of Esthetic: According to the Principles of St. Thomas Aquinas*, Washington, D.C.: The Catholic University Press, 1947, 118.

3. Wladyslaw Tatarkiewicz, *History of Aesthetics: Medieval Aesthetics*, trans. by R. M. Montgomery, Warsaw: PWN Polish Scientific Publishers, 1970, II, 3.

4. Benedetto Croce, *Aesthetic: A Science of Expression and General Linguistic*, trans. from the Italian by Douglas Ainslie, U.S.A.: Noonday Press, 1969, 175.

5. Tatarkiewicz, II, 3.

6. Ibid, 298.

7. Erwin Panofsky, *Abbot Suger: On the Abbey Church of St. Denis and Its Art Treasures*, Princeton: Princeton University Press, 1979, 278.

8. St. Bonaventure, *IV Sevtentiae*, D. 24a. 1 Q. 1 ad 3, 237.

9. Grosseteste, *Commentary on Pseudo-Dionysius" Divine Names*, IV, 230.

10. Thomas Aquinas, *Summa Theologica*, 1 q. 5a 4ad 1, 257.

11. Gerald Hawkins, *Stonehenge Decoded*, New York: Doubleday and Company, Inc., 1965. 166.

12. Pierre Teilhard de Chardin cited in Hawkins, 166.

13. Stephen Happel, "Lights and Mirrors: Stained Glass as Metaphors for the Catholic Soul," *Stained Glassin Catholic Philadelphia*, Jean Farnsworth, et al, eds. Philadelphia: St. Joseph University Press, 2002, 310.

14. John Fowles and Barry Brukoff, *The Enigma of Stonehenge*, Verona: Arnoldo Mandadori Editore, 1980, 18.

15. Leon E. Stover and Bruce King, *Stonehenge: The Indo-European Heritage*, Chicago: Nelson-Hall, Inc., Publishers, 1979, 181.

16. Michael Drayton, cited in Gerald S. Hawkins, *Stonehenge Decoded*, 167.

17. Fowles, 5.

18. Christopher Chippendale, *Stonehenge Complete*, New York: Cornell University Press, 1983, 10.

19. sarsen:. The sarsens are natural blocks of a kind of sandstone. In the Tertiary period, up to seventy million years ago, much of the chalk deposit, still lying on the seabed where it had been laid down, was covered with sand. In places the sand became firmly concreted into irregular blocks, and these remained when the chalk was raised into hills and the looser sand eroded away. These boulders are sarsens. The finest sarsen deposits are those on Marlborough Downs. Chippendale, 38.

20. Ibid., 14.

21. Horace Walpole, *Anecdotes of Painting*, cited in Stover and Kraig, ix.

22. Stover and Kraig, ix.

23. Siegfried Sasson, cited in Fowles, 127.

24. Ibid. 53.

25. Fowles,

26. Hawkins, 167.

27. Henry James, cited in Hawkins, 166-167.

28. From hereon, all quotations from the Bible, unless otherwise noted, will be taken from, Alexander Jones, gen. Ed., *The Jerusalem Bible*, New York: Doubleday and Company, Inc., 1966.

29. Tatarkiewicz, 16.

30. William L. MacDonald, *The Architecture of the Roman Empire: An Introductory Study*, Revised Edition, New Haven: Yale University Press, 1982, 121.

31. William L. MacDonald, *The Pantheon: Design, Meaning and Progeny*, Cambridge: The Harvard University Press, 1976, 13.

32. Ibid., 13.

33. B. W. Henderson, "Life and Principate of the Emperor Hadrian, *"Encyclopedic Dictionary of Religion*, Washington, D.C.: Corpus Publications, 1978, 1597.

34. Margurite Yyourcenar, *Hadrian's Memoirs*, cited in MacDonald, *The Pantheon*, 92.

35. orrery: an apparatus showing the relative positions and motions of bodies in the solar system by balls moved by clockwork. Webster, 1290.

36. MacDonald, *Pantheon*, 90.

37. Ibid. , 91,

38. Dio Cassius (Hist., LIII, 27) cited in Karl Lehmann, "The Dome of Heaven," *The Art Bulletin*, New York: The College Art Association of America, Vol. 27, 1945, 22.

39. MacDonald, *Architecture*, 120.

40. Ibid., 118.

41. Robert Wernick, "Fifteen Centuries Later, Ravenna's Mosaics Still Glow," *Smithsonian, January 1990*, 56.

42. Michael W. Cothren, "The Recollection of the Past is the Promise of the Future," Farnsworth, 2002, 10.

43. Charles H. Sherrill, *Mosaics,* London: John Lane the Bodley Head, Ltd., 1933, 3.

44. Giuseppe Bovini, *Ravenna*, New York: Harry N. Abrams, Inc., 1971, 12.

45. Cothren, 11.

46. Wernick, 57.

47. Stephen Happel, "Theology and the Visual Arts: Stained Glass as 'Windows' and 'Mirrors', Afterword, Farnsworth, 311.

48. Grosseteste, *Commentary on Pseudo-Dionysius' Divine Names*, IV, 230.

49. Harold Osborne, *Aesthetics and Art Theory: An Historical Introduction*, New York: E. P. Dutton and Company, Inc., 1970, 11.

50. Erwin Panofsky, "Classical Mythology in Medieval Art," *Metropolitan Museum Studies 4 (1932-1933)* 268.

51. William Fleming, *Arts and Ideas*, New York: Holt, Rinehart and Winston Publishers, 1980, 95.

52. Benedetto Croce, *Aesthetic: As Science of Expression and General Linguistic*, trans. from the Italian by Douglas Ainslie, U.S.A.: The Noonday Press, 1969, 175.

53. Tatarkiewicz, 30.

54. Frederick Heer, The *Intellectual History of Europe: The Medieval World: Europe 110-1350,* trans. from the German by Janet Sondheimer, New York: A Mentor Book, The New American Library, 1963, 381.

55. Madeline H. Caviness, "Preface," *Stained Glass Before 1540; An Annotated Bibliography,* Boston: 1983, xvii.

56. Erwin Panofsky, "Preface," *Abbot Suger on the Abbey Church of Saint-Denis and Its Art Treasures,* Princeton: Princeton University Press, 1946, vii.

57. Michael Cothren, "The Recollection of the Past Is the Promise of the Future," Farnsworth, 9.

58. Abbot Suger, cited in Tatarkeiwicz, 175-176.

59. Grosseteste in Tatarkiewicz, 227.

60. Panofsky, 208.

61. Suger, cited in Erwin Panofsky, ed., trans., and annotator, *Abbot Suger: On the Abbey Church of St.Denis and Its Art Treasures,* Princeton: Princeton University Press, 1979, 51.

62. Panofsky, p. 37.

63. Meyer Schapiro, *Romanesque Art,* New York: George Braziller Press, 1977, 11.

64. Paula Lieber Gerson, ed., *Abbot Suger and Saint-Denis,* New York: The Metropolitan Museum of Art, 1987,174.

65. Emile Male, *Religious Art in France in the Twelfth Century: A Study of the Origins of Medieval Iconography,* Princeton: Princeton University Press, 1978, 154.

66. Pseudo-Dionysius, *De coelesti hierarchia (Concerning heavenly hierarchy)* V. 3(PG 3, c. 121), 34.

67. anagogical: interpretation of a word, passage or text (as of Scripture or poetry) that finds beyond the literal, allegorical, and moral senses a fourth and ultimate spiritual or mystical sense. Webster, 63.

68. Erwin Panofsky, *Abbot Suger on the Abbey Church,* 2nd Edition 1979, *62-65.*

69. H.W. Janson, "Editor's Preface," in George Zarnecki, *Art of the Medieval World: Architecture, Sculpture, Painting the Sacred Arts,* New York: Harry Abrams, Inc., Publishers, 1975, 1.

70. Jerry Filteau, "Nation's First Catholic Cathedral to be Restored," *Newsfronts: The Florida Catholic,* April 24, 2003, A 24.

71. Filteau, A24.

72. Dag Hammarskjold

73. Dag Hammarskjold, taken from the quotation, which hangs outside the Meditation Chapel at the United Nations Building.

74 Adele Rowland, O.P. Statement taken from a 1983 questionnaire sent out by the author to many artists who happened to be a woman religious.

Works Cited

Aquinas, Thomas. *Summa Theologica,.*

Bonaventure, St. IV *Sevtentiae.*

Bovini, Giuseppe. *Ravenna.* New York: Harry N. Abrams, Inc., 1971.

Callahan, O.P. Leonard. *A Theory of Esthetic: According to the Principles of St. Thomas Aquinas.* Washington, D.C.: The Catholic University of America Press, 1947.

Caviness, Madeline H. "Preface," *Stained Glass Before 1540: An Annotated Bibliography.* Boston: 1983.

Chippendale, Christopher. *Stonehenge Complete.* New York: Cornell University Press, 1983.

Cothren, Michael W. "The Recollection of the Past is the Promise of the Future," in Farnsworth, *Stained Glass In Catholic Philadelphia.* Philadelphia: St. Joseph's University Press, 2002.

Croce, Benedetto. *Aesthetic: A Science of Expression and General Linguistic,* trans from the Italian by Douglas Ainslie. U.S.A.: Noonday Press, 1969.

Eco, Umberto. *Art and Beauty in the Middle Ages.* New Haven: Yale University Press, 1986.

Farnsworth, Jean, ed. *Stained Glass in Catholic Philadelphia.* Philadelphia: St. Joseph's University Press, 2002.

Filteau, Jerry, "Nation's First Catholic Cathedral to be Restored," in *Newsfronts: The Florida Catholic*, April 24, 2003, A 24.

Fleming, William. *Arts and Ideas.* New York: Holt, Rinehart and Winston Publishers, 1980.

Fowles, John and Brukoff, Barry. *The Enigma of Stonehenge.* Verona: Arnoldi Mandadori Editore, 1980.

Gerson, Paula Lieber, ed. *Abbot Suger and Saint-Denis.* New York: The Metropolitan Museum of Art, 1987.

Grosseteste. *Commentary on Pseudo-Dionysius' Divine Names, IV.*

Happel, Stephen, "Lights and Mirrors: Stained Glass as Metaphors for the Catholic Soul,," in *Stained Glass in Catholic Philadelphia,* in Farnsworth, ed. Philadelphia: St. Joseph University Press, 2002.

Hawkins, Gerald. *Stonehenge Decoded.* New York: Doubleday and Company, Inc., 1965.

Heer, Frederick. *The Intellectual History of Europe: The Medieval World: Europe 1100-1350.* New York: A Mentor Book, The New American Library, 1963.

Henderson, B .W. "Life and Principate of the Emperor Hadrian," *Encyclopedic Dictionary of Religion.* Washington, D.C.: Corpus Publications, 1978.

Janson, H.W. "Editor's Preface," in George Zarnecki, *Art of the Medieval World: Architecture, Sculpture, Painting the Sacred Art.* New York: Harry Abrams, Inc., Publishers, 1975.

Jones, Alexander, gen. ed. *The Jerusalem Bible.* New York: Doubleday and Company, Inc., 1966.

Lehmann, Karl, "The Dome of Heaven," *The Art Bulletin,* New York: The College Art Association of America, Vol. 27, 1945.

MacDonald, William L. *The Architecture of the Roman Empire: An Introductory Study,* Revised Edition. New Haven: Yale University Press, 1982.

_____ *The Pantheon: Design, Meaning and Progeny.* Cambridge: The Harvard University Press, 1976.

Male, Emile. *Religious Art in France in the Twelfth Century; A Study of the Origins of Medieval Iconography.* Princeton: Princeton University Press, 1978.

Osborne, Harold. *Aesthetics and Art Theory: An Historical Introduction.* New York: E. P. Dutton and Company, Inc., 1970.

Panofsky, Erwin, "Classical Mythology in Medieval Art," *Metropolitan Museum Studies 4 (1932-1933).*

Schapiro, Meyer. *Romanesque Art.* New York: George Braziller Press, 1977.

Stover, Leon E. and King, Bruce. *Stonehenge: The Indo-European Heritage.* Chicago: Nelson-Hall, Inc., Publishers, 1979.

Tatarkiewicz, Wladyslaw. *History of Aesthetics: Medieval Aesthetics,* trans. by R..M. Montgomery, Warsaw: PWN Polish Scientific Publishers, 1970.

Walpole, Horace, *Anecdotes of Painting,* cited in Stover and Kraig.

Yyourcenar, Margurite. *Hadrian's Memoirs,* cited in MacDonald, *The Pantheon.*

Chapter Three

Stones of Norwich, Ashes of Auschwitz:
Julian of Norwich and Etty Hillesum
Finding Wisdom by Praying Life Experience

Margie Thompson, SSJ

Foreword

They were obviously opposites: Julian, the medieval Catholic recluse meets Etty, the modern, bohemian, Jewish extrovert. Slowly, I *realized* the connections in the "hazelnut" version of each of their philosophies of life:

"All shall be well" (Julian of Norwich) and "Life is beautiful." (Etty Hillesum) I prayed to know the deeper connections between Etty Hillesum and Julian of Norwich. It was spring break, a few years ago, and I was in the house of a friend. Sipping my morning coffee, I prepared for prayer. My copy of *Rilke's Book of Hours: Love Poems to God*[1] lay in a basket beside my chair. I know from reading Etty Hillesum's diary[2] that she read Rilke regularly: "I always return to Rilke . . . for support and ready response to our bewildered questions." I opened the book randomly and read the poem, "God speaks to each of us as God made us"[3] Deep wisdom from lived experience resonated in my own heart. Amazed, I *realized* that I heard Etty's and Julian's voices in Rilke's words:

> God speaks to each of us as God made us,
> Then walks with us silently out of the night
> These are the words we dimly hear:
> You, sent out beyond your recall,
> go to the limits of your longing.
> Embody me:
> Flare up like flame
> And make big shadows I can move in.

Let everything happen to you: beauty and terror.
Just keep going. No feeling is final.
Don't lose yourself lose me.
Nearby is the country they call life.
You will know it be its seriousness.
Give me your hand.

Introduction

Two women from very different religious, cultural and historical contexts teach us surprisingly similar truths about God, prayer, and our human life. While Julian of Norwich teaches from years of theological reflection of her visions or "Showings," Etty Hillesum shows us God working through her reflections on her everyday life recorded in her diaries and letters. This essay explores these similar truths through the movement of Rilke's poem, "God speaks to each of us as God made us," which serves as the organizing principle for this research. This study begins by presenting the biography and *Sitz im Leben* of Julian of Norwich and Etty Hillesum. Each woman engages her given history, her life experience, prayerfully through her writing, which serves as her spiritual practice and reveals this engagement as wisdom spirituality.[4] Deeply attracted to God, Etty and Julian are drawn to profound depths of yearning and intimacy, finding within themselves a power to hold both mystery and contradiction. This power, however, was hard won. Each needed to wrestle with and through the process of her quest for God. Nevertheless, in this quest for God, each discovered God's quest for her. Both found God in suffering and suffering in God. What we learn from these two women is embodied prayer—that is, praying one's life experience.

God speaks to each of us as God made us,
then walks with us silently out of the night.

Julian of Norwich: Biographical Information

While we know much about the vision and thought of Julian of Norwich, the fourteenth-century anchoress, visionary, writer, and theologian, we know few details of her personal life. What we do know of Julian we glean primarily from her writings and from the history and customs of her time. She tells us that she was thirty-and-a-half years old when she wrote the short text of her "Showings." She lived the enclosed life of an anchoress, but had a maidservant to help her. She may also have enjoyed the company of a cat, as was customary for an anchoress at the time. Her anchor-hold was a cell adjoining the parish church of St. Julian—hence her name—in Conisford at Norwich. The cell opened onto a garden where Julian could take exercise, and a window opened onto the street so people could come to talk with the anchoress.

Julian's "window on the world" provided access to the ongoing human drama and the raw material for her theological reflection on the tender and merciful love of God. Julian lived in tumultuous times. As an anchoress, she listened to people at the window, heard of the tumult and miseries of the day, and gave spiritual advice. As a prayerful woman, she contemplated her unusual visions or showings to discern and deliver God's message. She listened, prayed, and thought. This was her ministry, her service to God and to God's people. Julian served as the discerning heart of Norwich.

Etty Hillesum: Biographical Information

We know much more about the life and times of Etty Hillesum than we do of Julian of Norwich. Etty was twenty-seven years old in 1941 when she began her diary, sitting at her desk, which she refers to as her "true hub,"[5] in her small room, which she loved. She lived in a house on Gabriel Metsustratt in South Amsterdam within an unconventional household of two women and three men who became her community of friends and lovers. Through Etty's writing, we become aware of the specific ways the German occupation of Holland and the Nazi program to eradicate the Jews affected the life of a vital, young, well-educated professional Jewish woman living in Amsterdam in 1941.

Through her regular journal entries, we witness the gradual constraints on normal life and mobility among the Dutch Jews. Eventually Etty's life became spatially confined to deportation barracks at Westerbork, the last stop before Auschwitz for more than 100,000 Jews. "Mud and misery were the essence of Westerbork—as were sickness and overcrowding—a universe of noise and fear crammed into a patch of heath half a kilometer square."[6]

In the end, Etty, like Julian, experienced the confinement of limited space that did not isolate her from the world around her, and did not shrivel her spirit but became, instead, an opportunity to develop an interior discipline and spirituality.

God speaks to each of us as God made us,
then walks with us silently out of the night.

Sitz im Leben: Black Death and Holocaust

Etty and Julian both became spiritual companions to people experiencing anguish and mortal danger. These women, too, lived in mortal danger. Etty lived in the life-threatening specter of German authorities, the squalor of the camp, her own poor health, the ubiquitous transport trains to the death camps, and the Holocaust. Julian was vulnerable to church authorities and the Inquisition, the Black Death which was sweeping through Europe and England, and poverty and squalor caused by the disease and the incessant wars.

Through the window of her anchor-hold, Julian witnessed the miseries of her world. She heard the heartbeat of a courteous God through the heartbreak of her townsfolk as she wrestled with the meaning of her visions. Hence her theological reflection informed her spiritual direction even as her listening informed her theology. Her theology is at once simple and profound, in touch with life, and encoded with compassion. She delivers a message of mercy and forgiveness from a most courteous God.

Etty's prayer too is colored with compassion as she listens in the dark night of Westerbork.

> At night, as I lay in the camp on my plank bed, surrounded by women and girls gently snoring, dreaming aloud, quietly sobbing, and tossing and turning, women and girls who often told me during the day, "we don't want to feel, otherwise we are sure to go out of our minds," I was sometimes filled with exquisite tenderness, and lay awake for hours letting all the many, too many impressions of a much-too-long day wash over me and I prayed, "Let me be the thinking heart of these barracks."[7]

These are the words we dimly hear.

Writing as Spiritual Practice

For Etty, as for Julian, the writing became a spiritual practice, but each woman used different processes. Etty used her writing to keep in touch with herself. "I must make sure I keep up with my writing, that is, with myself. . . ."[8] In fact, we discover Etty's life learnings as she does, as they gradually unfold in her diaries and letters. Her inner life is revealed in her writing; and her inner life is where God is waiting to reveal Godself.

Julian uses writing to discern and reveal the spiritual meaning of her revelations. Hence, Julian's writing is a well-organized theology, written in a masterful style; her writing is considered by some scholars to be comparable in quality with Chaucer's. She often develops her themes in parallel couplets and triplets. For example, in the Fourteenth Revelation of *Showings* Julian teaches about prayer: "I am the ground of your beseeching. First, it is my will that you should have it, and then I make you to wish it, and then I make you to beseech it."[9] In the same revelation she writes of mercy and of grace with similar elegance and precision:

> For I contemplated the property of mercy and I contemplated the property of grace, which have two ways of operating in one love. Mercy is a compassionate property, which belongs to motherhood and tender love; and grace is an honourable property, which belongs to royal dominion in the same love. Mercy works, protecting, enduring, vivifying, and healing, and it is all the tenderness of love; and grace works with mercy, raising, rewarding, endlessly exceeding what our love and labor deserve, distributing and displaying the vast plenty and generosity of God's royal dominion in his wonderful courtesy.[10]

While Julian's writings are the "Showings" of her accomplished theological thought presented as teachings for others, Etty's writings are less formal. Presented in the form of personal reflections in a writer's diary, they are, nevertheless, vital, immediate, and accomplished. The journals and letters served as the place where Etty came to know what she thought and believed from processing what she experienced. Etty's beloved room, desk, and diaries become a kind of anchor-hold for her interior life. Her journal entries explore and expose the wisdom of her life. They chart her spiritual growth and we witness her transformation. Eventually, Etty becomes Wisdom's messenger and minister.

You, sent out beyond your recall.

Writing as Wisdom Spirituality
Because writing became prayer and spiritual practice for Julian of Norwich and Etty Hillesum, we learn about life and prayer from them. By engaging the events of their lives, discerning the signs of their times, and tending to God's cordial and compelling presence encoded in them, these women honored their experience as the content of prayer. They practiced an ancient form of wisdom spirituality. By reflecting on their everyday human experience on a deep level, they met Divine Wisdom and lover her.

In the everyday experiences of growth and reflection . . . God is strikingly immanent. She "pervades and permeates all things." (Wisdom 7:24) This divine reality does not retreat into another realm, but is "spread out upon the world, and people just don't see it." (Gospel of Thomas 113) [11]

But Julian sees it. She records God's revelation of the "deep wisdom of the Trinity, our "Mother . . . who is working on us in various ways."

> God, all wisdom is our loving Mother with the love and goodness of the Holy Spirit, which is all one God . . . and the deep wisdom of the Trinity is our Mother. . . . And so our Mother is working on us in various ways, in whom our parts are kept undivided . . . our substance is in our Mother, God all wisdom. [12]

Through their writings, Julian and Etty both process their encounters with Wisdom, at the heart of life, "working on us in various ways." They present their learnings for our deeper reflection. Wisdom's message and fruits are evident in the clarity and energy of their words and their lives.

When one learns one taps into a power that is greater than one's self. When one seeks wisdom, one opens one's self to being changed and to growing. When one learns something one cannot go back to a former state of being. Wisdom propels one into newness. She makes all things new and bigger for those who follow her. [13]

Although Julian teaches us about prayer throughout her *Showings*, neither she nor Etty left detailed instructions on methods of prayer, as did Teresa of Avila or Ignatius of Loyola. However, in their writings, each woman models her engagement with her vision, her desire for Wisdom, and, ultimately, her intimacy with God.

Go to the limits of your longing.
Embody me.

Prayer as Attraction, Yearning, and Intimacy

Intimacy with God accounts for the simplicity of each woman's message. Intimacy with God colors the complex and painful path that led to profound truths: "All shall be well" and life, "Life is beautiful."

> At the end of each day I feel the need to say: Life is very good after all. I have my own philosophy now, one I'm prepared to speak up for, which is saying a lot for the self-conscious girl I've always been.[14]

Etty Hillesum, like Julian, knows a God so close to us we are wrapped in God-self as in our clothing. "He is the goodness of everything . . . our God, who has enclosed us all in himself." [15] Julian's portrait of God's intimate loving for us is specific and sensuous.

> For He does not despise what he has made. . . . For as the body is clad in cloth, the flesh in skin, and the bones in the flesh, and the heart in the trunk, so are we, soul and body, clad and enclosed in the goodness of God . . . always complete and closer to us, beyond any comparison. For truly our lover desires the soul to adhere to him with all its power . . . this pleases God most and soonest profits the soul.

In her Fourteenth Revelation, Julian teaches at length about prayer. She teaches that God is the source, the foundation, and the first receiver of our prayer. Julian exhorts us to fidelity in prayer, which she says is our "duty" and "obligation diligently to perform."

> And when we do it will seem to us that it is nothing. And this is true. But let us do what we can, and merely ask mercy and grace, and everything which is lacking in us we shall find in him. And this is what he means when he says: "I am the foundation of your beseeching."[16]

In her teaching about prayer, Julian speaks of dryness, gratitude, trust, and union with God. She characterizes true knowledge of God and the mutual desire of God and the beloved soul as the fruit of our prayer. She discusses union and contemplative prayer in sensuous and erotic terms of mutual desire.

> Therefore we pray to him urgently that he may do what is pleasing to him as if he were to say: How could you please me more than by entreating me, urgently, wisely and sincerely, to do the thing that I want to have done? And well I know that the more the soul sees of God, the more she desires him by grace.
> And so we shall by his sweet grace in our own meek continual prayer come into him now in this life by many secret touchings of sweet spiritual sights and feelings measured out to us as our simplicity may bear it. . . . And then we shall come into our Lord, knowing ourselves clearly and wholly possessing him, and we shall all be endlessly hidden in him, truly seeing and wholly feeling, and hearing himself spiritually and delectably smelling him and sweetly tasting him. And there we shall see him face to face, familiarly, wholly.[17]

Julian's images of God contrast sharply with the image of a justly wrathful God, all-present and all-knowing, that she was taught about through the church. Such a God was much like Job's God, making deals with Satan to "test us"[18] and find us worthy or unworthy. Therefore, the teaching of the day emphasized human unworthiness and sinfulness. Julian replaces this fearful God-image with a revelation of God as creator, protector, lover,[19] life, love, and light.

> In this matter I had touching, sight and feeling of three properties of God, in the strength and effect of all the revelation. . . . The properties are these: life, love and light. In life is wonderful familiarity, in love is gentle courtesy, and in light is endless nature. . . . I contemplated with reverent fear, greatly marveling at the sight and the feeling of sweet harmony.[20]

Etty comes gradually to know God in these properties of life, love, and light as well. Early in her diaries, Etty introduces herself as "the girl who could not kneel." Later, she talks most candidly about her own transformation into "the girl who learned to pray." "What a strange story, it really is my story: the girl who could not kneel. Or its variation, the girl who learned to pray. This is my most intimate gesture, more intimate even than being with a man."[21]

In an extended entry on October 9, 1942, Etty talks about prayer and love, sex and intimacy:

> I am going to read St. Augustine again. He is so austere and so fervent. And so full of simple devotion in his love letters to God. Truly those are the only love letters one ought to write: love letters to God. Is it very arrogant of me to say that I have too much love to give it all to just one person? Will people never learn that love brings so much more happiness and reward than sex? I fold my hands in a gesture that I have come to love, and in the dark I tell you silly and serious things and implore blessings upon your honest sweet head. Yes, I pray for you. Goodnight, beloved.[22] *Flare up like flame and make big shadows I can move in.*

Powerful Women: Hospitality to Mystery and Contradictions

In times of great affliction and human cruelty, Julian of Norwich and Etty Hillesum embodied a powerful love which held fast to mercy, refusing to hate or punish cruelty. They also enfleshed a huge hope which refused to despair in the face of disillusionment and destruction. They witnessed to a faithful God who remains present to her suffering one. What Gail Godwin said of Teilhard can be said of Etty and of Julian: "[their] hospitality to contradictions has embraced more and more of the universe until it admits the ultimate Guest who has been at the heart of things all along."[23]

Etty loved life and people with a passion. Of her own soul she wrote on October 12, 1942:

> Sometimes it bursts forth into full flame within me, as it has just done again: all the friendship and all the people I have known in the past year rise up in over-

whelming number and fill me with gratitude. And, though I am sick and anemic and more or less bedridden, every minute seems so full and so precious— what will it be like when I am healthy once more." "I rejoice and exult time and again, O God: I am grateful to You for having given me this life."[24]

Although she loved life, Etty did not accept the hiding places offered to her by several friends that might have saved her life. Others offered to work with influential connections to procure a deferment for her. These she also refused, choosing instead to return to the camp, to the friends she had made there. She returned to help the people there, especially the ill and the children, awaiting deportation to Poland.[25] Her intensity was often a danger to her health and well-being, but the largeness of her soul, the "soul work" she had commenced by her "wrestling with" her psychotherapist Julius Spier, her journaling, and her prayer allowed her to hold the tensions in balance.

September 28, 1942
True, I may think too much, with a demonic and ecstatic intensity, but I refresh myself from day to day at the original source, life itself, and I rest from time to time in prayer. And what those who say, "you live too intensely," do not know is that one can withdraw into a prayer as into a convent cell and leave again with renewed strength and with peace regained.[26]

Everywhere, Etty saw the horrors and the contradictions in her world, but she chose life and love within and, ultimately, beyond the contradictions.

Living and dying, sorrow and joy, the blisters on my exhausted feet and the jasmine behind the house, the persecution, the unspeakable horrors—it is all as one in me, and I accept it all as one mighty whole and begin to grasp it better if only for myself, without being able to explain to anyone else how it all hangs together.[27]
Let everything happen to you: beauty and terror.

Wrestling with Therapist and Vision

Etty's physical and psychological wrestling with her therapist Julius Spier and Julian's intellectual and spiritual wrestling with her vision of Christ Crucified and his bleeding head motivated these women to pray their way through the milieu of darkness of their everyday worlds into profound faith in God whom they experienced as person, wisdom, mercy, life, and love. Each of these women trusted her experience, committed herself to pursuing her vision, to wrestling with it, and to learning from it. In the process, each ultimately found her voice. Each woman expressed her faith in mantra-life refrain. For Julian, "All shall be well." For Etty, "Life is beautiful." How can we understand such optimism spoken by one facing down the Black Death of the plague and another the black smoke of the death camps?

Julian's vision of the crucified Jesus and his bleeding head both frightened and delighted her. She spent at least twenty years of her life wrestling with it and learning its meaning. She received her revelations in 1373 and concluded the writing of the long text in 1393. Julian gives a firsthand account of her visions beginning in the third chapter of *Showings*:

> And when I was thirty and a half years old, God sent me a bodily sickness in which I lay for three days and three nights, and on the third night I received all the rites of Holy Church and did not expect to live until day. . . . My curate was sent for to be present at my end. . . . He set the cross before my face, and . . . I agreed to fix my eyes on the face of the crucifix . . . and suddenly . . . all my pain was taken from me, and I was as sound as ever I was before. Then suddenly it came to my mind that I should wish for a second wound, as a gift and a grace. . . . And at this, suddenly, I saw the red blood running from under the crown, hot and flowing freely and copiously, a living stream, just as it was at the time when the crown of thorns pressed his blessed head. And at the same revelation, suddenly the Trinity filled my heart full of the greatest joy, and I understood that it will be so in heaven without end to all who will come here. God showed me this in the first vision and, God gave me the space and time to contemplate it. And then the bodily visions ceased, and the spiritual vision persisted in my understanding.

Julian's vision lasted throughout the day, numbering sixteen revelations in all. Julian accepts her responsibility to interpret the teachings correctly and even asks questions of God to be sure she understands. Soon after her vision Julian writes an account, now known as the "Short Text," so others might benefit from God's revelations to her which she believed were given to her for "all humans." A fruit of her vision and her prayer, then, is love for others and a concern to lead them to God.

> In all this I was greatly moved in love toward my fellow [humans], that they might all see and know the same as I saw, for I wished to be a comfort to them, for all this vision was shown for all humans. All this was shown in three parts, that is to say, by bodily vision and by words formed in my understanding, and by spiritual vision. But I may not and cannot show the spiritual visions as plainly and as fully as I should wish.[28]

Over the twenty years which transpired between her revelations and the completion of the long text of *Showings*, a good deal of Julian's wrestling with the visions was in her effort to resolve her "obsessive problem" of how "sin, damnation and the anger of God can be reconciled with . . . the loving workings of mercy and grace upon the soul."[29] Julian attempted to resolve this conflict in several ways. One was through the parable of the Lord and the servant in the fifth chapter, which shows how the relationship between God and humans can exist despite our frailty. In the eleventh chapter, Julian concludes that "sin is no thing,"[30] and in the twenty-seventh chapter, she contends, "Sin is necessary, but all will be well, and all will be well, and every kind of thing will be well. But I did not see sin, for I believe that is has no kind of substance, no share in being, nor can it be recognized except by the pain caused by it."[31] In her "conclusion" to the long text, Julian simply and profoundly resolves the meaning of the vision and of her own cognitive dissonance and finds rest from her wrestling: "For truly I saw our Lord's meaning, that he revealed it because he wants to have it better known than it is. . . . What, do you wish to know your Lord's meaning in this thing? Know it well; love was his meaning."[32]

Etty Hillesum began to write in her diary when she was twenty-seven, at the same time that she began seeing Julius Spier for psychotherapy sessions, hoping "He would bring order to my inner chaos, harness the forces now at loggerheads within me."[33] Etty was admittedly intense. She worked hard, through this relationship with Spier, to resolve her issues, especially relationship issues: her jealousies and possessiveness on the one hand and her desire for independence on the other. "Because she believed in him, Spier became her 'task,' the person against whom she tested and questioned herself, the occasion of her struggle and growth."[34] Spier became Etty's friend, spiritual mentor, and eventually, her lover. Her wrestling with Spier, though actually physical at first, became a metaphor for her dealing with the inner turmoil that this relationship stirred within her. "When we wrestled for the first time it was an enjoyable context, and though it was a little unexpected I immediately 'caught on:' I realized it was all part of the treatment."[35]

> But to go back, "Body and soul are one." That was no doubt why he began to test my physical strength in a sort of wrestling match. I was apparently more than adequate, for remarkably enough, I floored the man, big though he was. All my inner tensions, the bottled up forces, broke free, and there he lay, physically and also mentally, as he told me later, thrown. No one has ever been able to do that before, and he could not conceive how I managed it. His lip was bleeding.[36]

In this relationship Etty gained both a balance and an inner strength that fostered her awakening spirituality. It was through Spier's encouragement that she began to write regularly, recording the interior conversation that ultimately became her dialogue with God.

> Vanity of vanities—but what was not vain was my discovery that I was able to commit myself unreservedly to another, to bind myself to him and to share his sorrow. And did he not lead me to God, after paving the way with his imperfect human hand?[37]

Spier died on September 15, 1942, the same day that the Gestapo came to take him to Westerbork. When Spier died, Etty addressed him in her diary:

> There you lie now in your two small rooms, you dear, great, good man. . . . I had a thousand things to ask you and to learn from you, now I will have to do everything by myself. But I feel so strong that I'm sure I'll manage. What energies I possess have been set free inside me. You taught me to speak the name of God without embarrassment. You were the mediator between God and me, and

now you, the mediator have gone, and my path leads straight to God. It is right that it should be so. And I shall be the mediator for any other soul I can reach.[38]

Etty continued to wrestle with dramatic changes in her life. On July 29, 1942, she voluntarily accompanied the first group of Jews being sent to Westerbork camp. At the end of August she fell ill, probably from exhaustion and stress, and was given leave to return to Amsterdam for a few days. She stayed there for over a month because of her illness. Her last notes were written during the time after Spier's death on September 15 and reflect the time she had to deal with her life experiences. These last pages are filled with reflections on her life and her sickness, as well as on faith, God, prayer, and intimacy.

> I now realize, God, how much You have given me. So much that was beautiful and so much that was hard to bear. Yet, whenever I showed myself ready to bear it, the hard was directly transformed into something beautiful. And the beautiful was sometimes much harder to bear, so overpowering did it seem. To think that one small human heart can experience so much, O God, so much suffering and so much love, I am so grateful to You, God, for having chosen my heart, in these times, to experience all the things it has experienced.[39]

For Etty, the metaphor of wrestling, initiated by Spier, expands to incorporate her wrestling with the meaning of life itself. She wrestles with specters and visions, demons and fears, and the cold hard reality of the Nazi death camps. It was in this hellish grip that she wrote in her last letter from Westerbork written on September 2, 1943: "[W]e have become marked by suffering for a whole lifetime. And yet life in its unfathomable depths is so wonderfully good, Maria—I have to come back to that time and again. And if we just care enough, God is in safe hands with us despite everything, Maria."[40] Etty Hillesum died in Auschwitz on November 30, 1943.

Just keep going. No feeling is final.
Don't let yourself lose me.

God's Quest for Us: Our Quest for God

> And also our good Lord revealed that it is very greatly pleasing to him that a soul come naked openly and familiarly. For this is the loving yearning of the soul through the Holy Spirit. . . . God of your Goodness give me yourself, for you are enough for me, and I can ask for nothing which is less, which can pay you full worship. And if I ask anything which is less, always, I am in want; but only in you do I have everything.[41]

Through her teaching, Julian accepts responsibility to help God in God's quest for us, and to help us not to lose God. "In this working he wants us to be his helpers, giving all our intention to him . . . for I saw truly that our substance is in him."[42] Her revelations and her writings of the tender and merciful love of God serve to counteract the prevailing desolate teaching, through which the harshness of a punishing God convinces people of their unworthiness. "Then this was my astonishment, that I saw our Lord God showing no more blame to us than as if we were as pure and as holy as the angels in heaven."[43]

Julian's own longing, learned in her quest for God, describes well Etty's quest that began with yearning for inner peace and balance. "By true longing we are made worthy."[44] Totally engaged with her therapist and her healing process through her writing, Etty was led from neurotic self-absorption to total abandonment in love expressed as compassionate service to others in the face of the transport trains and the death camp of Auschwitz. Throughout her diaries and letters, we feel Etty's increasing quest for God, her growing inner strength, and her faith both in herself and in life.

> 25 February, 1942
> It is now half-past seven in the morning. I have clipped my toenails, drunk a mug of genuine Van Houten's cocoa, and had some bread and honey, all with what you might call abandon. I opened the Bible today . . . no answers . . . just as well because there were no questions, just the enormous faith and gratitude that life should be so beautiful, and that makes this a historic moment, that and not the fact that S and I are on our way to the Gestapo this morning.[45]

Here, too, we recognize that simplicity, openness, familiarity, and nakedness with which Etty approaches her life, her truth, and her God. Reading her diaries, we witness the attraction for God transformed to yearning, and ultimately to service and to union. "Alone in the middle of the night God and I have been left together, and I fell all the richer and at peace for it."[46] When we read her description of her "exquisite tenderness" for the women and girls in the barracks, we believe her; we believe that her union with God is so complete that it is God's tenderness for God's people that she is feeling. On October 4, 1942, Etty wrote of prayer: "One ought to pray day and night, for the thousands. One ought not to be without prayer for even a single minute."[47]

> One phrase has been haunting me for weeks now: "You must have the courage to say openly that you believe; to say 'God.' Right now, a little spent and tired and sad and not altogether satisfied with myself, I don't feel it with the same intensity, but it still remains part of me. Tonight I shall probably say nothing to God, although I do yearn for cold stone floors and contemplation and seriousness . . . I no longer plumb the depths of despair. . . . I know that those moments are too part of life's ebb and flow and that all is well.[48]

The openness to her own nature and her truth allow Etty to write with surprising honesty about the cruelty of the German plan, concluding, "The rottenness of others is in us too. . . . It is too easy to feel vindictive."[49] She witnessed and wrestled mightily with the demon named hate and yet she could write of an intellectual conversation with a friend: "Despite all the suffering and injustices, I cannot hate others."[50] Later, in a letter describing in graphic detail the existential situation of the camp at Westerbork, she holds to her refusal to add more hatred to the world:

> this is a very one-sided story. I could have told you quite another, filled with hatred, bitterness and rebellion . . . the absence of hatred in no way implies the absence of moral indignation. I know that those who hate have good reason to do so. But why should we have to choose the cheapest and easiest way? It has been brought forcefully home to me now that every atom of hatred added to the world makes it an even more inhospitable place. And I also believe . . . that the earth will become more habitable again only through that love that the Jew Paul described to the citizens of Corinth in the thirteenth chapter of his first letter.[51]

The Pauline passage to which Etty refers is the one on love, "If I speak in tongues of mortals and of angels and do not have love, I am a noisy gong or a clanging cymbal . . . and if I hand over my body to be burned and do not have love, I gain nothing."[52] The journey through Westerbork to Auschwitz was long, and was filled with very real doubt and terror as Etty saw the hatred in the faces of the Nazis guards at the camp. Her resolve to love in the face of that hatred did not keep her from struggling with questions concerning God's role and responsibility in the face of this terrible suffering. Her intimacy with God helps her resolve those questions.

> But one thing is becoming increasingly clear to me: that You cannot help us, that we must help You to help ourselves. And that is all we can manage these days and also all that really matters; that we safeguard that little piece of You, God, in ourselves. And perhaps in others as well. Alas, there doesn't seem to be much you yourself can do about our circumstances, about our lives. Neither do I hold you responsible. You cannot help us, but we must help You and defend Your dwelling place inside us to the last.[53]

In her last diary entry that has survived, October 13, 1942, Etty writes, "I have broken my body and shared it among men. And why not, they were hungry and had gone without for so long. . . . We must be willing to act as balm for all wounds."[54]

Nearby is the country they call life.
You will know it by its seriousness.

God and Suffering

Julian of Norwich and Etty Hillesum lived in two of the "worst of times" in European history. Julian witnessed the horrors of the Black Death, suffering from years of war, abuses in the church, and fear of the Inquisition. Etty witnessed the horrors of the Holocaust, fuelled by institutionalized Christian anti-Semitism and genocide.

Something has crystallized. I have looked our destruction, our miserable end, which has already begun in so many small ways in our daily life, straight in the eye, and accepted it into my life, my love of life has not been diminished. I am not bitter or rebellious or in any way discouraged. I continue to grow from day to day, even with the likelihood of destruction staring me in the face.[55]

Theologians have grappled with the problem of evil and the question of God after Auschwitz, the apparent ultimate dissolution of Christian civilization, and the resultant questioning of the Christian God. Feminists and liberation theologians question and critique the meaning of atonement soteriology as "divine child abuse."[56] What do we do with the question of God and suffering? Joseph Sievers reflects on Etty's amazing prayer in which she forgives God and resolves to "help God."

Etty writes in her diary that stupendous and disconcerting "Sunday morning prayer" in which she says among other things "Neither do I hold you responsible but later you will declare us responsible." This is a theology, a theodicy not made up of abstracts but which is born of the tragic experience of every day. Perhaps it is difficult logically to affirm that God needs help, needs to be forgiven, is not responsible for events. But we see how, in Etty, there is a seeking for God which is increasingly intense and profound. Christian influences, like kneeling to pray, are certainly present. Yet Etty poses the question of God in terms in which feeling co-responsible partners with God is sometimes expressed forcefully.[57]

In their writings about their experiences, Etty and Julian offer us, not an *idea* about God *and* suffering, but an *experience* of God *in suffering*; not a treatise on the *how* of prayer but the exposure of the *who* of prayer and of the *fruit* of prayer embodied in those experiences. Each woman gives a concrete example of how prayer inspires real people to live lives of loving service in response to their intimate experience of a God who is close to us and who suffers with us. Prayer led them to know this God. Their engagement with life experience as embodied prayer led them to listen with their hearts, to think with their hearts, and to love with their lives. Because of their engagement through writing, we can discern God's touch, God's merciful work, and God's great need.

We must only speak about the ultimate and most serious things in life when the words well up inside us as simply and naturally as water from a spring. And if God does not help me to go on, then I shall have to help God.[58] We remain alone, God and I, there is no longer anyone else who can help me.[59]

How might their image of a God who suffers with us affect our theology and praxis of prayer? How might an image of a tender, vulnerable God-with-us affect our sense of community and service?

I do not have many illusions about the way things really are, and I even renounce the pretext of helping others; I will always start with the principle of helping God as much as possible and if this works, so much the better because it means that I will also be helping others. But on this point I have no heroic illusions.[60]

Etty may have had no heroic illusions, but her embodied love took on heroic proportions and expanded her moral horizon. Her "deepest reaching out to others in love . . . points clearly to the enduring experience of humanity that love is central in moral life—a truth that can and must speak to us in our time."[61] Grounded in an experience of the love of God, Etty Hillesum and Julian of Norwich assume their responsibility to bear the burden of love and witness to the dynamic life of God at work in the world, particularized in each woman's response to the social concerns of her time.[62]

Give me your hand.

Conclusion

Two women from very different religious, cultural, and historical contexts teach us surprisingly similar truths about God, prayer, and our human life. Through their own words we learn "two ways of operating in one love."[63] In the face of the unimaginable miseries of their times, these mystical women did not escape into solitary contemplation but embodied their prayer as a listening heart and a loving presence, as witnesses to the power of mercy and forgiveness. Years of prayer and theological reflection on her experience of God through her visions and her window on the world taught Julian of Norwich that God is close, that mercy works, and that God's purpose and our own is the same: Love.[64] Etty Hillesum shows God working, first in her in her journey to her own self, and then through her as "the thinking heart of the barracks . . . willing to act as a balm for all wounds." They surely did not ignore the horror and miseries of their world. But Julian and Etty refused to focus on suffering, choosing instead to focus on love. The fruit of their love as peace and power, as astounding faith and joy, is recording in their writings. Their embodied prayer led to embodied Wisdom, and then to embodied love as care for others. It was *through* and not *in spite of* her life experiences that each woman found her unique voice, her central task, and her sensitive service as response in love to Love. "In this love we have our beginning, and all this shall we see in God without end."[65]

Notes

1. Anita Burrows and Johanna March (trans.), *Rilke's Book of Hours: Love Poems to God* (New York: Riverhead Books, 1996).

2. *Etty Hillesum: An Interrupted Life and Letters from Westerbork* (New York: Henry Holt and Company, 1996), p. 230. See also p. 170, Etty's diary entry on the afternoon of Tuesday, July 7, 1942: "I would like to read every thing of Rilke before the time comes when I won't perhaps be able to lay my hands on books for a long time. . . . To-

night I dreamed I had to pack my case. . . . And I had to find room somewhere for the Bible. And if possible for Rilke's Book of Hours and Letters to a Young Poet.

3. Rilke, *Book of Hours*, I, 59, p. 88.

4. Wisdom spirituality is a way of entering into relationship with the Divine through the process of reflection on one's human experience.

5. Hillesum, p. 121.

6. Ibid., p. xx.

7. Ibid, p. 225.

8. Ibid., p. 19.

9. Julian of Norwich, *Julian of Norwich: Showings* (New York: Paulist Press, 1978), p. 248.

10. Ibid., p. 262.

11. Hal Taussig, "In Every Thought She Comes to Meet You: The Spiritual Potential of Biblical Wisdom Literature, *Constellation: An Online Journal*, tcpc.org (2002), p. 6.

12. Julian of Norwich, pp. 293-294.

13. Taussig, p. 6.

14. Hillesum, p. 88.

15. Julian of Norwich, p. 186.

16. Ibid., pp. 249-253.

17. Ibid., pp. 254-255.

18. Job 1-2:7.

19. Julian of Norwich, p. 183.

20. Ibid., pp. 339-340.

21. Hillesum, p. 228.

22. Ibid.

23. Gail Godwin, *Heart: A Person Journey Through its Myths and Meanings* (New York: Morrow, 2001), distributed as a handout in a graduate course on spirituality.

24. Hillesum, p. 228.

25. Ibid., p. xii. Eva Hoffman poses a possible theory for Etty's refusal to take this help.

26. Ibid., p. 217.

27. Ibid., p. 154.

28. Julian of Norwich, pp. 179-187.

29. Ibid., p. 24.

30. Ibid., pp. 197-198.

31. Ibid., p.224.

32. Ibid., p.342.

33. Hillesum, p. 6.

34. Ibid., p. ix.

35. Ibid., pp. 20-23.

36. Ibid., p.6.

37. Ibid., p. 222.

38. Ibid., p. 200.

39. Ibid., p. 198.

40. Ibid., p. 359.

41. Ibid., p. 184.

42. Julian of Norwich, p. 292.

43. Ibid., p. 266.

44. Ibid., p. 244.

45. Hillesum, p. 85.
46. Ibid., p. 226.
47. Ibid., p. 226.
48. Ibid., p. 82-83.
49. Ibid., p. 84.
50. Ibid., p. 86.
51. Ibid., p. 256.
52. 1 Cor. 13.
53. Hillesum, p. 178.
54. Ibid., pp. 230-231.
55. Ibid., p. 155.

56. Joanne Carlson Brown and Rebecca Parker, "God so Loved the World?" in Carol J. Adams and Marie M. Fortune, Eds.,*Violence Against Women and Children:A Christian Theological Sourcebook* (New York: Continuum, 1995, pp. 36-59.

57. Joseph Sievers, "To Help God, Reflections on the Life and Thought of Etty Hillesum," *The SIDIC Periodical* (1992.3), www.sidic.org/Periodicals/95N3ind.htm.

58. Hillesum, P. 173.

59. Ibid., p. 192.

60. Ibid., p. 148.

61. Francis T. Hannafey, "Ethics as Transformative Love: The Moral World of Etty Hillesum," *Horizons* 28/1 (2001), pp. 68-80.

62. Thomas Kelly, *A Testament of Devotion* (San Francisco: Harper Collins, 1992).

63. Julian of Norwich, p. 262.

64. Ibid., p. 342, "What, do you wish to know God's meaning in this thing? Know it well, love was God's meaning. Who reveals it to you? Love. What did God reveal to you? Love. Why does God reveal it to you? For Love."

65. Ibid., p. 343.

Works Cited

Barrows, Anita and Johanna Macy, translators. *Rilke's Book of Hours: Love Poems to God*. New York: Riverhead Book, 1996.

Flinders, Carol Lee. *Enduring Grace*. San Francisco: Harper Collins, 1993.

Godwin, Gail. *Heart: A Personal Journey Through its Myths and Meanings*. New York: Morrow, 2001.

Hannafy, Francis T. "Ethics as Transformative Love: The Moral World of Etty Hillesum," *Horizons* 28/1 (2001), pp. 68-80.

Hillesum, Etty. *An Interrupted Life and Letters from Westerbork*. New York: Henry Holt and Company, 1996.

Julian of Norwich. *Julian of Norwick: Showings*. New York: Paulist Press, 1978.

Kelly, Thomas. *A Testament of Devotion*. San Francisco: Harper Collins, 1992.

Sievers, Joseph. "To Help God, Reflections on the Life and Thought of Etty Hillesum," *The SIDIC Periodical-1995.3.* www.sidic.org/Periodical/95N3ind.htm.

Taussig, Hal. "In Every Thought She Comes to Meet You: The Spiritual Potential of Biblical Wisdom Literature." *Constellation: An Online Journal.* March, 2002. www.tcpc.org.

Chapter Four

The Water That Shattered the Stone

Barbara Lonnquist

> Hearts with one purpose alone
> Through summer and winter seem
> Enchanted to a stone
> To trouble the living stream . . .
>
> Too long a sacrifice
> Can make a stone of the heart.
> O when may it suffice?
> > William Butler Yeats
> > *"Easter 1916"*

> Poor little brittle magic nation, dim of mind . . .
> . . . while elvery stream winds seling on for
> > to keep this barrel of bounty rolling
> . . . it is our hour or risings. Tickle, tickle,
> > Lotus spray.
> > James Joyce
> > *Finnegans Wake*

The physical and spiritual geography of Ireland has, from time immemorial, been predicated on the conjunction and opposition of water and stone. One look at the Cliffs of Mohr lashed by the Atlantic or at medieval monastic rock dwellings erected above bodies of water serves to remind us of the ironic marriage in Ireland of the solid and the fluid. The monasteries with their lakes and wells also testify to Ireland's dual heritage with its pre-Christian, Celtic past—the wells of its fertility cults converted literally into pools of baptism when Patrick brought the Church of Peter (whose name means Rock) to the island in the 5th century.

Archetypal images of stone and water, thus, naturally recur throughout Irish literary history, but the alternation between water and stone takes on added significance in literary representations of Ireland's quest for national identity—its struggle for "Home Rule" (independence from Britain) in the early twentieth century and its subsequent "troubles" generated by the Treaty that separated the six counties of the north from the Irish Republic.

This chapter will examine how three Irish authors writing across that twentieth century, namely Wiliam Butler Yeats, James Joyce, and contemporary novelist Edna O'Brien have used those archetypal symbols of rock and water to examine the dynamics of Irish history and, in particular, the narrative of Ireland's ongoing quest for an autonomous and integrated identity, even after the creation of an Irish Free state in 1921. Symbols of rigidity (stone) and freedom (water), these images also work as poetic reminders in Yeats, Joyce and O'Brien that the struggle against oppression occurs on two fronts: from without and from within, including a sometimes unholy collusion between internal institutions of church, state and family, the three "nets" Joyce's young artist, Stephen Dedalus, once said he most needed to flee. If flight has historically posed a problem to the Irish (the Flight of the Earls in the 17th century, dispossession through famine in the 19th century, and the exile of its artists in the 20th century), these three "Irish" authors, who wrote on and off the island, use literature to write to Ireland, to free it from within.

One thing among many that unites Yeats, Joyce and O'Brien is a critical understanding that history and narrative are more than a static memorializing of the past, but are rather, in their views and in literary practices, an active "remembering" of the past in the root sense of the word, that simultaneously plays its part in the creation of the future. Their respective bodies of work demonstrate how the way in which we narrate the past can affect—or more properly effect—its future. They also recognize the degree to which Irish poetry and politics have been conjoined in the creation and maintenance of Irish identity; in different ways, each of them invokes and continues that tradtion while resisting simplistic understandings of what national identity or a national literature means. Although the bulk of the chapter will center on Joyce, I will frame that discussion with two shorter analyses of a work by Yeats and one by O'Brien that employ the metaphorical opposition of water and stone relative to a seminal moment in Irish history, the Easter Uprising of 1916, and its long-term consequences throughout the century as history and as myth. The presence of Yeats and O' Brien also serves to elucidate Joyce's use of water and stone in the contrast between revolutionary singlemindedness and a more fluid, plurality of mindset.

Yeats' poem, "Easter 1916," cited in the epigraph above, serves as a case in point illustrating the complications attendant upon the union of Irish poetry and politics and the use of the metaphorical antithesis of water and stone within that context of a politically engaged, national literature. Despite Yeats' rejection of violence as a means of securing political independence, his poem, written in the weeks after the Easter Uprising (but not published until 1921) reluctantly acknowledges the transformation of Ireland in its wake: "All changed, changed utterly:/A terrible beauty is born." The now famous oxymoron, "terrible beauty," repeated three times as a refrain in the poem, which derives from Maude Gonne's recorded comment, "tragic dignity has returned to Ireland" (qtd. in Kiberd 216) also subtly suggests Yeats' divided mind toward the terror and heroism of blood sacrifice in the 1916 event (Kiberd 216). The leaders of the rebellion staged on April 24, 1916, whom he commemorates, were, upon execution by the British on May 3, 1916, turned into martyrs and thus they, along with Yeats, "resigned [their] part in the causal comedy." Yeats' allusion to theater here suggests his own anxiety about his complicity in the history of the event as poet and playwright. Yeats' role in the Uprising was not a direct one; nonetheless he felt that he played a remote part in the drama. His earlier works had invoked an idealism not unlike that pronounced by Patrick Pearse, the leader of the uprising, in calling men to arms.

Emer Nolan in *James Joyce and a Nationalism* (1995), describes the Easter Uprising as a surreal event staged by an odd amalgam of activist and poets:

> It was a revolution organized by myth-makers and poets: activists who could not even decide on what day the uprising was to take place, and some of whom had to interrupt their rehearsal of a play by W.B. Yeats to participate; insurgents who even forgot to bring the glue to paste up copies of their Proclmation of the Irish Republic. Indeed, no signed copy of the document exists and, in true Derridean style, there may never have been one; all copies were printed copies, the names of all the signatories printed reproductions. On Easter Monday morning, Patrick Pearse read the Proclamation from the steps of the GPO [General Post Office] to a largely indifferent crowd, many people attempting to go about their daily business as ususal. (133)

Yeats' play "Cathleen ni Houlihan," first produced in 1902 as part of the Celtic Revival, told the story of a young man who, on the eve of his wedding, forsakes material and romantic comfort to fight for the mythic figure of Mother Ireland appearing at his door in the guise of a poor old woman who has lost her four green fields, a common representation of Ireland under British rule in the "aisling tradition" of Irish poetry. Produced again in Dublin in the spring of 1916, in the weeks preceding the Easter Rebellion, it prompted Yeats to question the idealism of his earlier work celebrating Celtic mythic heroes, like the mighty Cuchulainn, when he saw the real-life cost for the young men who lost their lives when they marched against the British to die for Mother Ireland with little more than images of Cathleen ni Houlihan (who at the end of the play is transformed into "a young girl" with "the walk of a queen") and Pearse's Proclamation of "a nation once again" ringing in their ears.

Noting Yeats' divided consciousness in the poem, Declan Kiberd in *Inventing Ireland: The Literature of the Modern Nation* (1995), argues that the poem has two voices: "the public bard" (delivering the encomium), who was, according to Kiberd, "still trying to complete a poem which will please Maude Gonne" (the actress turned political radical for whom he had created the part of Cathleen ni Houlihan and with whom he had been and was still madly in love) and "the private lover . . . still hoping to cure her of *political rigidity*, urging her to forget *the stone* for the call of the moorcock" (216, emphasis mine). Kiberd argues for a multivalent reading of the poem that incorporates numerous responses to the Easter event, i.e., the rebels' supporters, those convinced of England's good will, pacifists opposed to violence, and ascendancy mockers (217). More tellingly though, Kiberd asserts that Yeats was a "national" and "not a nationalist poet" and thus the poem's "cliched tones" of patriotism at the end actually warn of the dangers of turning history in myth or worse, cliché:

> Wherever green is worn,
> Are changed, changed utterly
> A terrible beauty is born.

According to Kiberd, Yeats foresaw the hardening (my word choice) of the event into "a classroom cliché" in which "the rebels are changed but into *the fixity of heroes in a museum* " (217, emphasis mine).

Similarly, another critic notes that Yeats' use of the opposing imagery of water and stone "establishes two opposing concepts, one of life, full of dynamic and constant change, and its counterpart a lifeless embedded rock." This reading sees that the "living stream of pragmatism . . . the sights and sounds of the beauty of ever-changing nature" are in "endless conflict with the 'symbolic stone' of single-minded devotion to Irish nationalism ("1916" www.gmu.edu/org/ireland32/1916). The cultural aftermath of the uprising and Yeats poem is revealed, according to Richard Kearney author of "Myth and Terror" in the posters of the heroes that emerged throughout Dublin after Yeats'poem, one of which depicted Pearse "in a pieta position, supported by a tri-colour waving Mother Ireland" with the caption "All Is Changed" (qtd. in www.gmu.edu/org/ireland32/1916). When Pearse surrendered to the British, he predicted that the Irish would win their victory "in death." This echoes imagery Pearse had employed a year before his own death, speaking at the graveside of another rebel hero, O'Donovan Rossa: "Life springs from death and from the graves of patriot men and woman spring living waters" (qtd. in www.gmu.edu/org/ ireland32/1916). Yeats was, no doubt, aware of these words as he employed images of water and stone to counterpoint dynamic life versus a patriotism that exalts the grave.

The grave consequences of such fixity—whether political, cultural or religious—are emphasized throughout the work of James Joyce, from his first announcement of "paralysis" as his theme in *Dubliners* to his joking pun on the Latin of Church ritual: "Petrificationibus" [let us all be petrified, turned into stone] in the final section of *Finnegans Wake* (610) (which section I will argue below can be seen as a re-writing of the Easter Uprising). One could describe the trajectory of Joyce's literary production—a trajectory that was always more circular than linear—as moving from a realistic, even naturalistic, exposure of Ireland's "paralysis" in his early works *Dubliners* (1904-1906, published 1915) and *Stephen Hero*, the unpublished pre-text to *Portrait of the Artist as a Young Man*(1915) to his later representation of history as perpetual metamorphosis rendered thematically and stylistically in *Ulysses* (1922)[1] and realized directly in a fluid plot that replicates the contours of a dream in *Finnegans Wake* (1939)—a text that begins with and returns to the watery opening, "riverrun past Eve and Adam's"[an actual church on the River Liffy and creation in Genesis]. The *Wake* is a tragi-comic retelling of human and Irish history in the dreaming mind of a drunken father H.C.E., a.k.a."Here Comes Everybody," identified geographically with a mountain, and of his marriage to A.L.P., Anna Livia Plurabell, whose name and actions mirror the River Liffey.

Joyce's expressed purpose in writing *Dubliners* was to expose the petrified state of life in Dublin. This is recorded in two letters: one in 1904, to Constantine Curran as Joyce was beginning composition, "I call the series Dubliners to betray the soul of that *hemiplegia or paralysis* which many consider a city"(*Letters*, I, 55) and his well-known letter of July, 1906, to his prospective publisher at the time, Grant Richards, in which Joyce asserted, "My intention was to write a chapter in the moral history of my country and I chose Dublin for the scene because that city seemed to me to be the centre of paralysis"(*Letters*, II 134). Another way to describe the evolution from *Dubliners* to the *Wake* would be as a movement from gravity (literally, the seriousness of the grave) in *Dubliners* which opens with a funeral and ends with a story entitled "The Dead," to the the levity of constant wordplay, especially bi-lingual punning, which achieves a proliferation or even globalization of meaning, celebrating what Joyce calls "plurability" a quality associated with the feminine in the *Wake*. A.L. P's chapter begins "In the name of Anna the Allmaziful, the Everliving, the Bringer of **Plurabilities**, haloed be her eve, her singtime sung, her rill [brook] be run, unhemmed as it is uneven" (FW 104, my emphasis). ALP herself is introduced "bi-culturally:" the rhythm of the Our Father is detected by Christians ["thy kingdom come, thy will be done"] and the opening of the Quoran, ["In the name of Allah the all merciful'] by Muslims!

Unlike the prodigious word play in the *Wake*, there is little real humor in the lives of the Dubliners we meet in Joyce's debut liteary production. When laughter does occur, it is sometimes described as "mirthless" and the puns are, more often than not, lost on the characters, as in the example of the pun in the malaprop "rheumatic" – a paralyzed substitute for "pneumatic" in "The Sisters," as will be discussed below. Missing words are, in fact, the form of history represented in "The Sisters," the introductory story, which serves as a program piece for the recurring theme of paralysis in the collection. In its opening, the first-person narrator, a young boy, who has been tutored by a priest named Father James Flynn, is confronted by news of the priest's imminent death due to a stroke—"his third" (3). As the boy muses on the priest's condition, he turns the word over in his mind and mouth: "Everynight as I gazed at the [priest's] window I said softly to myself the word *paralysis*. It had always sounded strangely in my ears, like the word gnomon in the Euclid and simony in the Catechism.

But now it sounded to me like the name of some maleficent and sinful being" (3). His consideration of this mysterious, evil condition is amplified by a conversation between adults (significantly full of ellipses), into which he enters as he descends the stairs to supper. A neighbor, Old Cotter, is speaking to the boy's uncle:

-No, I wouldn't say he was exactly . . . but there was something queer . . . there was something uncanny about him. I'll tell you my opinion
-I have my own theory about it, he said. I think it was one of those . . . peculiar cases . . . But it's hard to say

The uncle, taking notice of the boy's entrance, replies:
-The youngster and he were great friends. The old chap taught him a great deal, mind you; and they say he had a great wish for him.
-God have mercy on his soul, said my aunt piously (4).

Ellipses run throughout the story; later, for example, when the boy and his aunt visit the Flynn home to pay their respects to the priest waked upstairs, the aunt and the sisters will speak with similar ellipses, avoiding the main subject of the story itself, death: "Did he . . . peacefully?" the aunt will ask. The title, "The Sisters," is itself an elliptical displacement of the main subject, Father Flynn. Such ellipses not only signal the reader to pay attention to the meaningful gaps in Joyce's text, but illustrate a repressed version of history that Jocye considered paralyzing to the young in Ireland.

In these debut stories, the young artist Joyce attempted to navigate between two versions of history that he was simultaneously trying to expose: the romantic excess of the Celtic revival, personified by Yeats and Lady Gregory (although it is clear in "Easter 1916," that Yeats questions such excess of devotion: "what if excess of love/ bewildered them") as well as the dangers of its antithesis, the repressed histories promulgated by the Catholic Church. Contemporary critics, reading "The Sisters" against the background of the clergy abuse scandal in American and Irish Catholicism, have interrogated the unspoken, or "unspeakable" story of Father Flynn, to cite Wilde's phrase (his trial took place the same year as Father Flynn's death which Joyce specifies as July 1, 1895). These readers have been alert to hints of repressed sexuality in Cotter's word "queer"—a more commonplace term in colloquial Irish of the past than its sexually specific reference today.[2] In Vicki Mahaffey's forthcoming work on modernism, she argues that the potential abuse in the story occurs at an intellectual level. Mindful of the cliché, "A mind is a terrible thing to waste," I would add that the child-prodigy in Joyce would have been keenly sensitive to the psychic blight inflicted on the psychic development of children by intellectually and culturally repressive institutions. In fact, I would argue that in *Dubliners,* Joyce critiques the power of the Church, which in the political vacuum of a colonial state, virtually substituted for civil authority, with power over the family, and thus promoted on two levels its gospel of repression.

For example, Eveline in the story of that title, another narrative of verbal repressions, is the victim not only of domestic abuse but of a pervasive culture of self-sacrifice, on both a nationalist and religious level, that discouraged young women from seeking freedom or opportunity abroad. The choice Eveline faces is between "going across the waters" (emigration) for a life of freedom with Frank, whose name means historically both honest and free (OED),[3] or being turned to stone at home in Ireland. Eveline's father who bans her from seeing Frank is also becoming increasingly violent. Her awarenss of this is juxtaposed with memories of her mother's tragic fate, suggesting a history of mistreatment of women:

> She would not be treated as her mother had been. Even now, though she was over nineteen, she sometimes felt herself in danger of her father's violence. She knew it was that that had given her the palpitations. When they were growing up he had never gone for her like he used to go for Harry and Ernest because she was a girl; but latterly he had begun to threaten her and say what he would do to her only for her dead mother's sake. And now she had nobody to protect her. (33)

Such behavior takes place in a house, where, enshrined above a symbolically "broken harmonium," is a "yellowing photograph of a priest (name forgotten), whom Eveline memorializes with the funereal sounding, 'He is in Melbourne now'"[4] beside "a coloured print of the promises made to Blessed Margaret Mary Alacoque" (30)—one of which was ironically the blessing of the home, which implied domestic harmony.

Despite Eveline's desire for "escape," she has been too indoctrinated by the rhetoric of "duty" (her mother made a deathbed plea for her "to keep the home together as long as she could" (33) and also, according to Katherine Mullin in "Don't Cry for Me Argentina: 'Eveline' and the Seductions of Emigration Propaganda") by a campaign of nationalist propaganda, often preached from the altar, warning against the sexual dangers of emigration for young women (182-189) Thus when it comes time for her to depart for a new life in Buenos Ayres with her fiancée Frank, she is literally frozen in stone, unable to move. The destination "Buenos Ayres," which is Spanish for "good air," stands in opposition to the repeated imagery of dust, a symbol of death: "Home . . . she looked around at all the familiar objects which she had dusted once a week for so many years, wondering where on earth all the dust comes from" (29-30). Dust here is a domestic, feminine variation in the larger motif of "dear dirty Dublin" threading throughout the stories of male hopes of freedom. Even more significantly though, in regard to the opposition of water and stone, is the lesser known religious origin of the name: "Buenos Ayres" also bears the now historically-eclipsed meaning of "good winds." Explorers for Spain in the time of Columbus would have prayed before their departure at the chapel of Ferdinand and Isabella in Seville before a portrait of "Our Lady of the Good Winds" to deliver them safely across and later back across the waters. (I recall my own surprise at discovering this portrait when visting the Royal Palace in Seville during a James Joyce Conference in 1994 and thinking what light it shed on Joyce's story!) The hidden implication of energy in her desired destination stands in marked contrast to Dublin and her own lack of agency when, at the end of the narrative, she is paralyzed by sudden terror that Frank would "drown" instead of "save" her as she romantically envisioned earlier that evening, and praying "to God to direct her, to show her what was her duty" (33), she grips the iron railing "passive, like a helpless animal (34) disabled by the nationalist and familial loyalties embedded in parables of "duty" and self-sacrifice (34). In Mullin's historicist reading of "Eveline" as a story of "thwarted emigration" at the turn of the century, she notes that Joyce was commissioned by George Russell to write a story for *The Irish Homestead*, a paper known for its didactic stories adhering to nationalist propaganda that "displacement from Ireland was dangerous" (172). If, as Joyce's biographer records, Russell promised Joyce "some easily earned money if you could write for the common understanding and liking for once" (qtd in Mullin 172), Joyce's narrative reveals instead "his estrangement from the kind of nationalism *The Irish Homestead* expected its stories to dictate"(Mullin 172).

If Eveline at age twenty has been disabled by Irish Catholic variations on the Victorian cult of the "the angel in the house"—a position accepted by the self-sacrificing sisters who act as Father Flynn's caretakers in "The Sisters," Joyce, at least, strips such ideals of the sentimentality with which they were invested in his time. Eveline's memorialization of her mother's tragic existence is spoken in a moment of pure terror, which is also her one moment of absolute clarity: she calls it "that life of commonplace sacrifice ending in final craziness" (32). It is also the only moment in the story we ever see Eveline move physically as she stands up in terror, shocked out of her ruminating by the window with dusty curtains. The terror of her mother's life which "laid its spell upon the quick of her being" moves her to announce: "Escape! She must escape! Frank would save her"(32). But Frank cannot liberate her from the hold the past has on her. Her epiphany about her mother's sacrificial life would be echoed seventy years after Joyce's composition at the conclusion of Edna O'Brien's story, "A Scandalous Woman"(1974), whose narrator states: "I realized that ours indeed was a land of shame, a land of murder and a land of strange, throttled, sacrificial women." Blood sacrifice, Joyce and O'Brien know, is not limited to war.

Joyce's narrator in "The Sisters," however, is still young enough—and as a male, he stood a somewhat better chance of escaping the gospel of repression that "laid its spell on the very quick of [Eveline's] being"(32). In fact, if one can imagine a positive epiphany on the boy after the narrative ends (and it ends midsentence), it would be of an alternative spell, produced by balancing his memories and intuition with what he overhears from the adults. This epiphany will yield itself if the boy (as well as the reader) can weigh the difference between the conventional lessons imparted by the priest-mentor in the boy's lifetime with the contrasting vision suggested by his posthumous "appearances" in the narrative.

The morning after Father Flynn's death, the boy tells us that before falling to sleep the previous evening, "In the dark of my room I imagined I saw again the heavy grey face of the paralytic. I drew the blankest over my head and tried to think of Christmas. But the grey face still followed me. It murmured; and I understood it had something to confess"(3). Later that day as he passes the Flynn home on Great Britain Street, (a hint of the oppressive alliance between Church and State) he confirms for himself the news of the priest's death by reading the notice on the door. Lacking the courage to go in and see for himself, he crosses to the sunny side of the street and is surprised to discover in himself "a senstion of freedom as if I had been freed from something by his death" (4).

As he reviews his tutorial sessions with his mentor who had studied at the Irish college in Rome he is retrospectively impressed not so much by the wealth of his knowledge (athough he recalls how his Uncle told Cotter that "the priest had taught him a great deal"(5) as by its gravity:

> he had taught me to pronounce Latin properly. He had told me stories about Napoleon Bonaparte, and he had explained to me the meaning of the different ceremonies of the Mass and of the different vestments worn by the priest. Sometimes he amused himself by asking me what one should do in certain circumstances or whether such and such sins were mortal or venial or only imperfections. His questions showed me how complex and mysterious were certain institutions of the Church which I had always regarded as the simplest acts. The duties of the priest toward the Eucharist and toward the secrecy of the confessional seemed *so grave* to me that I wondered how anybody had ever found the courage to undertake them; and I was not surprised when he told me that the fathers of the Church had written books as thick as the *Post Office Directory* and as closely printed as the law notices in the newspaper, elucidating all these intricate questions. (5 emphasis added)

And while the priest would sometimes "smile" or "nod his head" at the child's answers to his interrogation, such benignity is undercut by the boy's visual memory of his use of snuff and uncovering "big discoloured teeth" while letting "his tongue lie on his lower lip"—gestures that made the boy vaguely uncomfortable, and ones that foreshadow the physical reaction had by the boy in the the following story, "An Encounter," as he listens to the sleazy repetition of certain words, innocent in themselves, by a pederast.

The word "grave" in the extended quotation above signals a verbal motif that links the boy's association of the seriousness of the Church's moral pedagogy—that tends to overwhelm or paralyze him—with the grave of death. The priest's sister Eliza will explain Father Flynn's seriousness as his being "too scrupulous always. The duties of the priesthood was too much for him"(9). This meaning of "grave" in the context of scrupulosity recalls the Pauline distinction in 2 Corinthians 3:6 between "the letter of the law, which kills, and the spirit of the law, which gives life."

The missing component of "spirit" in an oppressive code of canon law, implied by "books as thick as the *Post Office Directory*" or the fine print of the "law notices in the newspaper," is underscored later that evening when the boy visits the Flynn house with his aunt and Eliza recounts how "poor James" had wanted to take them out for a drive in the spring in "one of them new-fangled carriages . . . with the rhematic wheels"(9). Eliza's malaprop, which substitutes "rhematic" for "pneumatic"—the name for new air-filled tires in 1895,—points to her and "poor" James' state of "paralysis" (as a rheumatic condition) and by omission suggests what is missing in their lives, namely the life-giving energy embedded in the Greek root "pneuma" which means both spirit and air. (The reference to air links this with the meaning in Buones Ayres). St. Paul's distinction in 2 Corinthians, furthermore, follows a reference to the old covenant as "laws written in stone" as opposed to the living law written in the human heart.

The sense of gravity as a burden that wears one down is mirrored by the boy's impression when, distracted during the sisters' muttering of prayers at the bedside of the corpse, he notices that one sister's cloth boots were "trodden down"(7). His "fancy" that "the priest was smiling as he lay there in his coffin" bespeaks perhaps his need for the "escape" of levity. But this proves wrong on closer inspection: "I saw that he was not smiling. There he lay solemn and co-pious, vested as for the altar, his large hands loosely retaining a chalice. His face was very truculent, grey and massive"(6). The ironic resemblance between this actual view with his dream the night before will be reinforced by a reference to the confessional when Eliza reveals the secret or unspoken story behind Father James' apparent queerness.

The occluded story about Father James comes out in Eliza's musings below, to which the boy covertly listens as he did with Cotter's remarks the night before. As if awakening from her "commuing with the past" Eliza suddenly says "shrewdly:" "Mind you, I noticed there was something queer come over him latterly." And again, she changes direction or tone: "He was too scrupulous always. The duties of the priesthood was too much for him. And then his life was, you might say crossed" and after a long pause she adds, "It was the chalice he broke . . . That was the beginning of it. Of course they say it was all right, that it contained nothing, I mean. But still . . . They say it was the [altar]boy's fault. But poor James was so nervous. God be merciful to him"(10).

Eliza continues with a vague explanation of how "that affected his mind" and he would go "wandering about" until one night when he couldn't be found anywhere, they thought to search the church and discovered him "sitting up by himself in the dark in his confession box, wide awake and laughing-like softly to himself"(10). After another pregnant pause, in which all of them listen, as if for Father James to speak for himself, Eliza repeats, "wide awake and laughing like to himself . . . so then of course, when they saw that, that made them think there was something gone wrong with him "(10).

The story, not wholly unexpectedly, ends on that ellipsis, which is also part denial; his laughter "made *them*"—not her—"think there was somehitng gone wrong with him." This is not unlike Eveline's denial of her father's abuse when she thinks "he was becoming old lately, he would miss her" (32) or her euphe-mism for his alcoholism as *"fairly bad* of a Saturday night" (31). The elliptical ending of the sister's narrative leaves the boy in the position of having to piece together for himself—and weigh the value—of the fragmented information he has received from the adults and to navigate between their implications and de- nials as he balances them against his own emerging powers of intuition or moral judgment. It seems significant that the boy surmised from his dream the priest's need to confess and the final laughter is set in a confessional. Although this scene has been read as evidence of a sexual sin, [5] it seems to me—and here I do not want to be guilty of the denial enacted thoughout the narrative—that the "grave" matter, "the maleficent and sinful being" of paralysis as the boy names it, is that not only the paralysis of which the priest is a victim but that which he and the Church perpetuated and perpetrated by burdening a child's spirit (emo- tion and intellect) with an unhealthy sense of scrupulosity, which is a form of paralysis.[6] The "mortal sin" of the tale, to use the priest's terminology against himself (mortal suggesting both human and inclined toward the grave) would thus be a form of spiritual or psychological murder. In Eveline's case such scrupulosity resulted in a displaced and paralyzing sense of "duty" to a "home" that was no longer intact (the children were grown, leaving only an abusve fa- ther who stole her earnings to drink) at the expense of her duty to herself. In *Joyce and the Law of the Father,* Frances Restuccia analyzes the "legacy of pun- ishment" which Joyce inherited from his "Dublin fathers and Catholic Fa- thers"(6). Restuccia catalogues the portraits of childhood drawn by Joyce that are filled with fathers (biological and clerical) who prohibit play (2-18). Eveline recalls how her father used to "hunt them out of the field with his blackthorne stick" when they were playing (*Dubliners* 29); the pandybat scene of the priest beating Stephen Dedalus in the classroom in *Portrait of the Artist* is a famous example. Restuccia draws a verbal connection between "the pedagogy of pun- ishment" and "pederasty" in this context: in *Portrait,* she notes that Stephen recalls "his sense of 'queer, quiet pleasure' in the priest's white, fattish, clean, strong, gentle yet sadistic hands"(Restuccia 11).

What Restuccia and many others have shown is that in *Portrait* and beyond, Joyce converts the pandybats and blackthorn sticks of oppressive fathers into the pen of word play. The missing element of play or humor—the root of which, Joyce demonstrates in the *Wake*—derives from moisture (as in humus, fertile soil). If humor cannot literally shatter the stone, it can, by its faculty for revers- ing the straightforward or the serious, offer an alternative view and thus help to re-vise that which has been written in stone. The priest's laughter, posthumously revealed, could be read not simply as tragic or crazed, but, coming as it does on the heels of the boy's intuition that the priest had something to confess, a poten- tial warning that taking the law so gravely brings death.

An important influence on Joyce's representation of childhood in *Dubliners* was the mystical and politically radical English poet, William Blake. In his po- ems about London's oppressed children–chimney sweepers or orphaned wards of corrupt church guardians—Blake adopted the persona of the prophet Ezechiel recording the misery of Londoners' "mind forged manacles" or, as in "The

Chimney Sweeper," he becomes the angel appearing in a dream to a young chimney sweeper who thinks of his life as a "coffin of black":"

> And by came an angel who had a bright key
> And he open'd the coffins and set them all free
> Then down a green plain, leaping laughing they run
> And wash in a river and shine in the sun
> Then naked and white, all their bags left behind
> They rise upon clouds and sport in the wind

The dream of children playing freely, the imagery an echo of the Book of Revelation, is Blake's vision of the future for children in England. It is, however, not the vision adopted by the speaker of the poem, an older chimney sweeper who ends the poem with the moral: "So if all do their duty, they need not fear harm." Such false counsel seems central to Joyce's understanding of generational cycles of paralysis. Similarly, Blake's "Urizen," the god of law, was a circumscribing figure much like the Dublin fathers who limited the "horizons" of their subjects. Despite the bleakness of Joyce's own vision in *Dubliners* with its notable lack of humor, its punning, although hardly sanguine, pointed the way for Joyce to achieve liberation, at least on a verbal level, through word play in his later work. This culminates in what French literary theorists have noted as the "jouissance" (joyance), or as Jacques Derrida punned, the "Joyce-ance" of the endless play in *Finnegans Wake*.

The recorso (final book) of the *Wake*, opening with the rising sun of Easter Morning, is Joyce's rewriting of Irish history and particularly the Easter Uprising. In the opening call to rise up: "O Rally! O rally!" we hear a potential echo of Patrick Pearse's call to arms in 1916. As "dawnfire" spreads "seeds of light" over a petrified Irish landscape, we see a "tablestoane" [tablets of law] at the center of a circle of ancient "macroliths" and "horned cairns." Even the Wellington Monument, honoring the Irish expatriate who defeated Napoleon, which sits in Phoenix Park (another echo of a rising and a reminder of the Phoenix Park Murders, the terrorist plot against England carried out by the Invincibles n 1882), is transformed into "vellumtones muniment" [stone tablets transformed into tomes of merriment] (595-596). The spectacle of monumentality, associated with masculinity and war in the text—earlier referred to as "monuments"— is counterpointed by a weather report predicting the return of revitalizing moisture, a feminine symbol associated with ALP: "the torporature is returning to normal. Humid nature is feeling itself freely at ease with the all fresco"(597). This is followed by a parody of morning prayer addressed to Padma, [the lotus, water lily of the Nile], which tenders humor as a fertile power that can undo the petrification of the past: "It is our hour or risings [a triple pun on Easter Rising, "orisons" (prayer) and "rison" French, let us laugh]. The prayer concludes with a conjunction of play, pray and spray: "Tickle, tickle let us spray" (597).

As the chapter moves in the register of A.L.P's voice, her laughing waters (Hiawatha) going back into the sea, it confronts the landscape-history of Irish sorrow "our lake lamented, our greyt lack, the city of Is is" and issues the imperative, "Lough" [Celtic for lake and German for laugh]. This is a different response to sorrow than war—and this is published in Europe as Germany was waging World War II. On the final page, as A.L.P is dispossessed of language, her final river of words merge into the sea, with a lisping kiss and a key given to H.C.E.: "Lps. The keys to. Given!" She, like Eliza in "The Sisters," leaves her sentence unfinished: "A way a lone a last a loved a long the" The dangling sentence with its final word only an article "the" (Joyce joked it was the weakest of grammatical parts) leaves the reader to continue writing the story or to return, laughingly, to try again to navigate his circular text, "rivverrun past Eve and Adam's "

Edna O'Brien's literary landscape has traditionally been the land of Irish girlhood in the west of Ireland. Her debut, *The Country Girls Trilogy* (1960-1964), earned her the reputation of being a female Joyce, whose sexually explicit themes were also banned in Ireland. After thirty years of prodigious output in novels and short stories, she made what seemed at first a radical departure from the world of female tales of love, love lost, love thwarted, and so on, into the underworld of I.R.A. politics and terrorism in her 1994 novel *House of Splendid Isolation*. In a narrative that moves back and forth between past and present, an older widow living alone, Josie O'Meara, is taken hostage in her once splendid house—its "battered history" (218) an image of Ireland itself. The escaped I.R.A. gunman who invades this space is McGreevey, a legendary figure known throughout the police force as either "the Cuchuliann" or "the sicko."

There will not be space to do full justice to the novel here, but it deserves discussion as an important companion piece to the motif of water and stone, which O'Brien acknowledges intertextually as a legacy from Yeats and Joyce, and also because of the connection it draws between the the politics of terrorism as the punishing legacy of the Easter 1916 event (or myth) and the domestic mistreatment of women and children as another part of Ireland's murderous, patriarchal past. O'Brien offers a courageous exploration of the dynamics that motivate and sustain terrorism as an unbreechable wall hardening humans into camps, from which they project the enemy as "the Other." Against a landscape of "carnage," of graves and mounds and more graves," the unborn child who concludes O'Brien's novel explains her daring purpose:

It weeps, the land does, and small wonder. [. . .] As the killer is close to him whom he kills. That's in a book. But to be close in body or bayonet is not enough. To go in, within, is the bloodiest journey of all. Inside, you get to know—that the same blood and the same tears drop from the enemy as from the self, though not always in the same proportion. To go right into the heart of the hate and the wrong and to sup from it and be supped. It does not say that in the books. That is the future knowledge. The knowledge that is to be. (232)

This unborn child, who frames the text in its opening and closing, represents the past and the future: those who have been lost in the blood sacrifice generated by a culture of brutality and those not yet born who will inherit this legacy. O'Brien writes for the future in this novel; if her narrative cannot "realize" concretely a world where hatred stops, it tries to imagine a way, a "knowledge" not yet "in the books" (232).

In his essay, "Outside History: Edna O'Brien's *House of Splendid Isolation*," Michael Harris describes the novel's "postmodern" resemblance to "pastiche" in its assemblage of letters, diary entries, snippets of poetry, songs, mythology, interspersed among the sections of the narrative proper that cut away like cinematic scenes (111). Like Joyce, O'Brien asks the reader to create a new future by assembling the fragments of history; like Yeats, she reveals how political conflict, informed by a mythology of idealism, must be deconstructed in order to make way for a more livable future. Besides the masculine echoes of Cuchulain, O'Brien invokes the memory of Easter 1916 to interrogate the relationship between modern terrorism and an allegedly more heroic past and to reissue Yeats' poignant question in the poem: "O when may it suffice?"

The echo of "1916," with its questions of who are the heroes and who are the terrorists, recurs throughout the novel, as demonstrated by a conversation between two guards awaiting Mc Greevy's capture: "But if you'd been in 1916, you'd be on their [the I.R.A.'s] side" to which the other replies: "That's different, that's a totally different ballgame. These guys are without conscience, without ideals and with only one proclamation, money and guns, murder, guns and money."   And his partner responds, "It's a sad thing, all the same"(202). By the time we read this conversation, we too have become intimate enough with McGreevey to know that such easy assignations of hero or villain are not sufficient.

As the novel questions the distinction between the bloodlust of the terrorist and that of the detective hot on his trail, it throws in a third player in Ireland's history of violence: the abusive husband. Thus as Josie's fate links with McGreevey's we see through flashbacks her brutal and infertile marriage to Jamie O'Meara, an IRA man killed in action. Led by the solitude of being held hostage in her house with a man for the first time in years, Josie relives her own past; she also becomes privy to McGreevey's sorrows—despite his seeming impenetrable wall of defense—which gives a human face to the terrorist. Toni Morrison once said of stories of some really difficult crime such as the incest in *The Bluest Eye*, "Since why is difficult to handle, one must take refuge in how." Her distinction aptly fits O 'Brien's method. Yeats' insight, "Too long a sacrifice/ Can make a stone of the heart," is central to O'Brien's exploration of the "how" of terrorism.

To take us, as the uborn child says, "right into the heart of the hate," O'Brien also shows us those moments where hearts, hardened by experience, feel the melting forces of "memory and desire," in Eliot's famous phrase. In our second sighting of McGreevy, even before we know his name, he is hiding in the manger of a stranger's barn with a rifle next to his chest, half asleep (reliving his child's funeral) and half waiting for the guards, when he is suddenly disturbed by the sound of a cow in labor. After cursing, "What the feck," he calls to

her: "Where are you, Peg . . . Peg?" Why he calls her Peg he did not know"
(15). Realizing that the calf is caught, he saves her, placing his own hands into
the mothers's canal to grip the calf's shins. As he sees her emerge, "A grey,
jeelyish stripling in a sack of grey" and "wipes the slime from her face," he
watches as "she feels her legs, flexes herself, hardening to the wonder of life."
When he sees the mother licking her "with such happiness" he thinks: "After all
that agony, the love, the impossible licking love of it"(16). This scene reveals a
side of McGreevy not shown in the previous television bulletin of his escape nor
even seen by Josie herself. This is the McGreevy that no one, but the reader,
sees. Even the farmer who enters minutes later has not seen it, but recognizing
what favor McGreevy has done him, and sensing who he is, he threatens his
wife with violence if she dares to call the police (17-19).

Memory and desire also rouse Josie, the alleged victim, to unaccustomed
action. Gradually we piece together the story of her unsuccessful emigration to
the U.S., where she was a maid in New York, her return to Ireland to work in
her uncle's pub as the chastened old maid, and her unexpected opportunity to
marry an Irishman with an elegant house. Only James, wounded by his own
past, cannot love her and uses sex as a way to control her, to ride her like a
horse, and to create children. Josie, we later discover, secretly aborts the child
conceived in brutality. Enter McGreevy, years after all this, Joise thinks, has
been put to rest. Josie does not actually fall in love with McGreevy. However,
their stories intertwine in such a way that she is able to accept and forgive both
of their pasts. One sorrow she relives is of an aborted friendship (while in the
throes of her loveless marriage) with a young priest, who visits their house.
Taken by the eloquence of his descriptions of the spring thaw in the Swiss
mountains, "water gushing in and out between the rills and valley, the flowers,
violet excresences being born out of the seams of rock" (144), Josie recalls,
desire welled up in her like a "river wild and rapid . . . swishing the lining of her
body"(159). Their relationship never prospers beyond words, but she is punished
for it, nevertheless, when a young farmhand, Paud (later an IRA informer, re-
named Padraig after Patrick Pearse) sees her waiting for him. (That her vigil was
to no avail, neither Paud nor her husband ever knew). But Jamie beat her that
night, "Zanily, he beat her for the pleasures he had not given her"(147).

McGreevey who has steeled himself to take any heat (or cold) does not melt
easily. Progressing from silent cohabitation, to political disagreement, to mutual,
if imperfect, understanding is the movment of their narrative; it is also the plot
of Irish history in the twentieth century. The final scene of reawakened desire
occurs just before McGreevy's capture. Having left for a mission, he now returns to the house. Significantly, it is freezing out, and against orders, he accepts
a hot toddy from Josie. This night they speak personally. When earlier that
evening she asked about his wife and child, he resisted: "Let her not wring out
of me things that belong soley to me" (196). Now she asks again and, softened
by the toddy and warmth, he admits his desire to be home, in the north; that he
would like "Warmth and food and company . . . but the British Army is in our

streets and it's wrong" (206). (Earlier he had described what it had felt like "to grow up in hate [in the north] to have been papist leper scum"(121). At this moment the sound of two wasps in the curtain puts him on alert. After they release the wasps into the cold air, "so beautiful, so piercing," they become garrulous, leading Josie to return to questions about his wife and child, to go to what she thinks is "the hidden source of him" (208). She taunts his patriotism, "The Ireland you're chasing is a dream," to which he replies, " No one in their right mind wants my life and I am in my right mind"(208). When he defends his isolation, "We have no one for us, only ourselves" (an echo of the motto of the Irish party, Sinn Fein), his voice becomes "low and lonely and liturgical"(209). Josie had earlier recalled her return to Ireland after the Civil War in the 1920s, "to help to put it right. Yes, those sentiments had risen up in her then and were still there, like spores lurking "(91).

In the next scene, Joise is cutting her hair, recalling he told her that "when the fight was over and the country one, he would like children, wains. It did not seem untruthful when he said it, but it did not seem as if it would ever be. And as she heard him say it, a great lunatic fork of longing rose up in her, to be young again to have wains (210). "'That's why I'm cutting my hair,' she says to the dying light inside her and the shadows in the room, 'to a world rushing away with not much time for the old and not that much for the young either'"(210). She puts a strand of her hair in a box marked TO BE OPENED AFTER MY DEATH; the box also contains her confession of her abortion years ago. Unfortunately her shorn hair makes the guards stationed outside think there are two men in the house when they shoot her on her way down the next morning to plead for McGreevy.

The expected "epic" showdown between "the Cuchlainn" and the detective Rory, (his name, a heroic allusion), "two supremos who had tracked each other like polar animals" (226) is after this, mere anticlimax, exhausted of its heroic energy. What the novel has achieved, however, is that two strangers (male and female; victim and victimizer) each locked in political, emotional death, experience the pull of human understanding across a huge chasm, and as a result feel the desire to give birth to a better future. When the unborn child, speaking from its grave, forgives Josie at the end, one feels that one grave stone, at least, has been rolled back. I see now that this chapter has been, like others in the collection, about children—children of war, children of oppression, children who will grow up (or not) to inherit our world. Yeats, Joyce, O'Brien, writing across time and space, remind us that the lessons of Irish history are not only for Ireland. They speak to us today. They challenge us about tomorrow.

Notes

1. Leopold Bloom, the hero of the novel is asked by his wife how to pronounce "metamorphosis" when she encounters it in a book. Her exasperated response to the word is ironically "O Rocks!" Also every episode of the novel has a different style—thus a constant metamorphosis.

2. Most recently Margot Norris in "The Gnomon of the Book: *The Sisters*," questions what the gaps and ellipses hide in this story. Norris offers a brief history of "innocent readings" of the story as well readings that have worked to "uncover" hidden suggestions of a more preadatory side to Father Flynn. For a full discussion of the hidden homosexual subtext of the story see Leonard Albert, ""Gnomonology: Joyce's *The Sisters*." *James Jocye Quarterly* 27.2 (1990):353-364. Leonard identifies many of the hidden codes for homosexuality in the story. He argues, for instance that the draper shop run by the sisters suggests covering up through words. One word which Leonard takes on as a cover or drape is the word "simony," which the young boy associates with the word "paralysis." Leonard poses that this name for a spiritual sin could also be a cover for the word "sodomy." The boy's attention to the physical sounds of the words he repeats in the opening of the story makes Leonard's theory that the three syllable words could be connected quite possible. Central to both Leonard's and Norris's readings is the word "gnomon," which the boys also associates with "paralysis." A gnomon is a geometric figure, a parallelogram from which a smaller parallelogram has been cut out. My reading does not deny the possibility of a sexual subtect in the story; nor do I think I am performing what Norris calls an "innocent reading." I am trying to emphasize the horror of traumatizing children through a pedagogy or theology of repression.

3. The modern understanding of frank as "honest" or "candid" derives from its earlier sense of a Frank as a free-man with the right to speak freely. The "Frankish"conquerors in early France were the only free men. In English "Franklin" was the surname of a freeman or landholder, thus Ben Franklin. As a verb, to "frank" a letter meant to allow it "free" postage or "free passage"—an echo that fits what Frank offers Eveline as well.

4. I am indebted to Alexandra Scheirer, a student in the honors program at Chestnut Hill College, for this "funereal" reading of the phrase, "He is in Melbourne now." She astutely heard in it an echo of the remark ofen made when someone has died: "He's in a better place now." Given Joyce's insistence that we should read with our ears as well as our eyes, this was right on the mark. Also, emigration was, for those who remained, often thought of as a death. The farewell party, when there was one, was called a "wake."

5. The section repeats the hints of sexual indiscretion suggested by the coded term "queer" used by Old Cotter and here adds the term "wandering" which was code for homosexuality in the late nineteenth century by association with Oscar Wilde, who, after his trial in 1895, adopted the name Sebastian Melmoth from the gothic novel, *Melmoth the Wanderer* (1820) by C.R. Maturin. (See *The Oxford Companion to English Literaure*). Margot Norris questions about this section: "What is the broken chalice a symptom of . . . ? One of the priest's strokes? Or the discovery of some misconduct on the part of the altar boy? The holes in the innocent readings continually open up the possibility of the unwhlolesome" (26).

6. Norris discusses Brian Bremen's attention to the theme of scrupulosity in the story citing its definition from the *New Catholic Encyclopedia*: "Scruples render one incapable of making with finality the daily decisions of life. The psychic impotence, providing a strady source of anxiety and indeciveness, is especially prevalent in ethical and pseudo-ethical areas" (qtd. in Norris, 22).

Works Cited

Primary Sources

Blake, William. "Chimney Sweeper." Songs of Innocence and Songs of Experience (1894). *The Norton Anthology of English Literature.* Volume 2. Seventh Edition. New York: Norton, 2000.

Joyce, James. *Dubliners* (1914). New York: Penguin Classics, 1992.

- - - *Finnegans Wake* (1939) New York: Viking Press, 1947.

O'Brien. Edna. *House of Splendid Isolation* (1994). New York: Penguin Plume, 1995.

- - - "A Scandalous Woman" (1974). *A Fanatic Heart: Selected stories of Edna O'Brien.* New York: New American Library, 1985.

Yeats, William Butler. "Easter 1916." *The Yeats Reader: A Portable Compendium of Poetry, Drama and Fiction.* Ed. Richard J. Finneran. New York: Scribner, 1997.

Secondary Sources

Albert, Leonard. "Gnomonology: Joyce's 'The Sisters'." *James Joyce Quarterly* 27.2 (1990): 335-346.

Harris, Michael. "Outside History: Edna O'Brien's *House of Splendid Isolation.*" *New Hibernia Review* 10.1(2006):111-122.

Kiberd, Declan. *Inventing Ireland: the Literature of the Modern Nation.* Cambridge, MA: Harvard UP, 1995.

Mullin, Katherine. "Don't Cry for Me Argentina: 'Eveline' and the Seductions of Emigration Propaganda." *Semi-Colonial Joyce.* Eds. Derek Attridge and Marjorie Howes. Cambridge: Cambridge UP, 2000.

Nolan, Emer. *James Joyce and Nationalism.* London: Routledge, 1995.

Norris, Margot. *Suspicious Readings of Joyce's Dubliners.* Philadelphia: U Pennsylvania P, 2003.

Restuccia, Frances, L. *Joyce and the Law of the Father.* New Haven: Yale UP, 1989. "1916." *The Journal.* Ireland 32. http://gmu.edu/org/ireland 32/1916_essay.html

Chapter Five

Warming the Stone Heart of a Child in Foster Care

Nancy DeCesare, I.H.M.

Introduction

Each day we are reminded of the countless inadequacies of the American foster care system. National and local news coverage confirms our deepest suspicions. Major parts of a system designed to offer comprehensive services to children including loving homes, trained foster parents and comprehensive medical and mental health services, all of which are in need of repair. Although all of these components are critical to the success of the foster care placement, mental health services are an essential aspect of the Child Welfare System offering children an opportunity for wholeness and healing.

Children and adolescents in this flawed foster care system are often left to the discretion of a dysfunctional family court system, and to caseworkers who are overwhelmed by large caseloads. The system suffers from insufficient levels of funding, including the provision of dollars for mental health services, and declining numbers of appropriate foster homes, group homes and residential programs. These problems are increasing at a time when more and more children and adolescents require stable, loving foster parents, community-based group homes and, at times, highly structured residential treatment centers with each type of placement offering a systematic, coordinated approach to the delivery of mental health services. This approach should include a provision that a child entering care receives a comprehensive mental health screening from a trained professional and recommendations for meeting the ongoing mental health needs of the foster child.

In a national survey of child welfare agencies, researchers found that assessments of mental health problems are not performed even though there is considerable evidence that there are high rates of developmental and emotional disorders among the foster care population (Landsverk et. Al., 2001). It is estimated that 35 to 50 percent of children in care have relational, coping skill difficulties and school failures due to emotional and behavioral disturbances that can range from moderate to severe (Landsverk, et. Al., 2001). Despite these statistics, researchers have found that it is highly improbable that foster children will receive adequate mental health services under the current system of managed care arrangements (Halfon et al., 1992; Harman et. al., 2000; U.S. DHHS, 2000a).

If we are to assist children and youth in foster care to cope with their loss and pain, mental health providers, bolstered by professional staff in the child welfare system, must leave no stone unturned to improve access to mental health services. These services must include an early comprehensive mental health screening, diagnosis and treatment, and better coordination of mental health services between mental health professionals and child welfare agencies (Webb & Harden, 2003). An array of mental health services should include therapeutic foster homes, community-based services, residential and day programs, and outpatient treatment. Each unique service can contribute to a comprehensive mental health program through which children and youth can begin a journey of hope and discover healing. By addressing the bitter hurts and wounds of the past, counseling professionals can help to soften the stone heart of a child or adolescent in foster care.

Scope of the Problem

There are currently over 500,000 children in the United States who reside in some form of foster care (C.W.L.A., 2004). A number of studies have concluded that between 50 to 80 percent of these children suffer from moderate to severe mental health problems (dosReis et al. 2001: Halfon et al., 2002). These numbers have dramatically increased over the past ten years, yet funding for mental health services has not kept pace with children's mental health needs, needs which appear more complex than ever (American Academy of Child and Adolescent Psychiatry, 2002). Even where mental health services are available, there are significant gaps in assessing the developmental and behavioral problems of children in foster care (Leslie, et. al, 2003). One of the major gaps in services is the lack of clear agency policies to assess the physical, mental, developmental and behavioral problems of children in care as well as to access community mental health resources (Leslie, et. al., 2003).

Half of all children in foster care are placed there because of abuse and/or neglect (most often at the hands of their parents); others may suffer moderate to severe behavioral problems including conduct disorders, difficulties in school, depression, addictions and impaired social relationships (Leslie, et. al., 2003). Research shows that children and youth in foster care are more likely to use mental health services when available than those children who are not in care (Leslie, et. al., 2003).

Parental alcohol and drug abuse is yet another factor in the foster care placement of children. Seventy-five percent of these children have parents who are directly involved in some form of substance abuse (Children's Defense Fund, 2003). Many of these children will remain longer in care as parents are wait-listed for drug treatment programs.

Some children enter the foster care system because they are medically fragile and/or physically handicapped. The parents of many of these children struggle with financial hardships or other physical and mental difficulties which prevent them from caring for a sick child; thus, placing them in care is their only alternative.

Currently, 24 percent of children entering the foster care system are coming into care for the first time and range in age from birth through five years (U.S. Department of Health and Human Services, 2003). The largest population of foster care children is youth between the ages of eleven and fifteen; they represent 160, 419 or 30 percent of the total (U.S.D.H.H.S., 2003).

Children in care come from many different racial and ethnic groups. African American children comprise 40 percent of our current foster care population followed by Caucasians at 33 percent, Hispanics at 12 percent and 4 percent from other racial/ethnic groups (C.W.L.A. 2003). There are slightly more males, (52 percent) than females, (48 percent) (U.S.D.H.H.S., 2003).

Most children will eventually be returned to their parents, but children with severe mental, emotional, behavioral or developmental problems may require a longer stay. These children are more likely to remain in placement, be moved from placement to placement, and have difficulties with being adopted (U.S.D.H.H.S., 2003). Two out of three children will return to their families in less than two years, but a significant number will remain behind, awaiting adoption or some other form of permanency planning (C.W.L.A 2003).

The child who is older, and who suffers from severe emotional and behavioral problems, is more likely to linger in the foster care system as he/she is moved from one level of care to the next. This will include movement from a community-based foster home to a community-based group home, followed by a three-month stay in a diagnostic center with the final placement recommendation being a highly structured residential treatment center. As the child, now adolescent, moves from one level of care to the next, he often experiences multiple schools, peer groups, caregivers, case workers and, at times, a lack of consistent nurturing and care with each new placement. These multiple variations and adjustments do not provide a cornerstone for the development of a stable, safe and loving environment in which to develop a loving sense of self and others, nor does this process provide for a coordinated approach to the delivery of mental health services.

These adolescents can be considered high risk as they struggle to sustain relationships in an environment which is often filled with disruptions, unpredictable gaps in services, changing caregivers, and a lack of permanent and safe housing. Research on adolescents in foster care indicates that there is a "high prevalence of psychopathology" among adolescents when this population is compared to those who have similar backgrounds but are not in care (dosReis et al., 2001). The high rate of psychopathology is not surprising given feelings of loss and separation from biological parents, confirmed and unconfirmed experiences of abuse and neglect, and the number of disruptions that adolescents often experience while in care. These ongoing troubling experiences and the trauma associated with each new placement cause unhealthy physical, spiritual, emotional and mental health dysfunction, hence, the "stone heart" syndrome. There must be a less disruptive and more coordinated approach to the delivery of care for these children that will include ongoing professional mental health services.

Psychopathology in Foster Care

Psychopathology is defined as the study of psychological disorders. Early childhood experiences often lay the foundation for specific psychological disorders, including borderline personality disorder, posttraumatic stress disorder (sometimes linked to Attention Deficit Disorder), and a host of other disorders often referred to as Pervasive Developmental Disorders. The latter may include Asperger's Disorder, autism, and the emergence of schizophrenia in adulthood (Aiello, 1999).

An extensive history of physical and sexual abuse, emotional and physical neglect, ongoing deprivation, lack of adequate food and housing, the frequency of mixed messages and lack of consistent and stable parental models all provide a foundation for acute mental illness. Many adolescents in foster care have had a broad history of multiple traumatic life experiences. These often include being victims of physical neglect, sexual abuse, or emotional abuse. Without substantive physical, emotional, spiritual and psychological mental health support, these negative experiences can cause not only difficulty with physical closeness, touching, intimacy, and trust, but the emergence of an impaired and damaged psyche.

The provision for intensive psychological treatment for children in foster care is sometimes challenging to arrange. Foster care children and adolescents are often moved from one temporary placement to another according to the availability of adequate or less than adequate foster homes or group homes. It is not uncommon for children and adolescents entering the foster care system for the first time, or changing foster homes or group homes because of behavioral problems, to spend days or even weeks in temporary housing. At times the foster care placement can be provided in an emergency shelter made available by the state where children and adolescents will remain during the day with night-time hours being spent in one foster home after another, according to availability, until such time as a more permanent placement is found.

A litany of emergency placements is not uncommon for adolescents with severe mental health problems, given their inability to tolerate the demands of intimacy and close family and small-group living. This constant mobility and lack of consistency for severely troubled adolescents does not provide the permanence needed to begin the healing process. In fact, it is not unusual for these adolescents to refuse to unpack their clothing as they begin to know innately that their stay will be short-lived. These frequent disruptions in placement often feed their depression, poor self-esteem, sexual acting out, drug and alcohol abuse and a host of other untreated negative behaviors. For many, these behaviors are the only way they can defend themselves against the suffering each has experienced. Often these adolescents internalize their pain and create avenues of acting out that will prevent adults from reaching them. Acting out may come in the form of running away for days on end, engaging in sexual promiscuity, substance abuse, self-mutilation, and many other ill-defined behaviors that can only lead to more desolation. Filled with despair, these adolescents build walls of steel and harden their hearts like stones, never wishing to allow another human being into their lives.

The following case study broadly illustrates one adolescent's journey through the foster care system taken from the author's thirty-year experience as a social worker in child welfare. The case material has been concealed to protect the confidentiality of the client.

Like many children in long-term foster care, the adolescent identified struggled with many aspects of his person including long-term goals, ongoing relationships, and multiple behavior problems. He is typical of adolescents who are moved over and over in a foster care system that is struggling to meet the emotional, physical and mental health needs of those it is designed to serve.

Case Example: A Conduct Disordered Child

This placement is the third foster care placement for twelve-year-old Adam. He was originally placed in foster care at the age of two because of his parents' alcohol abuse and neglect of him and his younger sibling. Both children were returned to their parents after 18 months in care and the parents' completion of a required outpatient substance abuse program.

The second placement for Adam came six years later after a violent domestic abuse arrest. The parents were found guilty of assaulting each other with kitchen knives. As a result, both spent several days in the hospital recovering from abdominal wounds. The children witnessed these stabbings. Late on the night of the altercation, the children were removed by Child Protective Services and placed with a foster family. This second separation lasted six months.

The third placement came when Adam was in seventh grade. His natural father was send to federal prison for mail fraud and while there he was diagnosed with cancer. Despite several surgeries during his imprisonment, he died of cancer two years after the initial diagnosis.

Adam's natural mother reported that the reason for this placement stemmed from the fact that Adam had been out of control since her husband's incarceration and death. Her efforts to keep the family together by applying for food stamps, welfare assistance and permanent housing had proved ineffective. In addition, the mother had suddenly and inexplicably become deaf, a condition her physician told her was permanent.

Adam gave a somewhat different reason for placement. He explained that his mother had a problem with "drinking" and that he often saw her intoxicated. She drank openly in front of him and would send him to purchase alcohol for her although he knew that he would not be served.

Records indicate that Adam was distressed over his home situation. He missed his father and was angry with his mother because of her constant drinking. He did not get along well with his younger sibling who remained with the mother. The fact that the mother placed this child apart from her and chose to keep the younger sibling at home exacerbated the problem.

After one visit home, Adam reported that his mother was running around the apartment complex naked and had to be subdued by a security guard. At first, the child stated that he found his mother's behavior funny but quickly changed his mind and stated that he was embarrassed for her and their family since some of his peers witnessed the incident.

Because of the mother's excessive drinking, lack of adequate supervision and the potential for major additional problems, the courts suspended Adam's unsupervised home visits. The mother rarely visited Adam, despite her stated intention to do so. This inconsistency has left the child with a great deal of hostility and anger towards her. This lack of visitation lasted over eight months until the mother's sudden death. A neighbor found her dead in her bed. An autopsy later revealed that she died of a cerebral aneurysm.

Adam's mother had requested to be cremated. Her son said that he wanted to be the person to set the body on fire. It took Adam's therapist many consistent sessions to convince the boy that he could not do this. A constant fascination with fire and burning became a common theme in Adam's life.

Adam's relationship with his house parents in a group home was a stormy one. He was generally suspicious of authority figures as reflected by his frequent requests to know "what's going on and why do I have to do it this way?" He appeared to be interested in impressing the house parents by using swear words and giving detailed accounts of his activities in the community which often included bullying and threatening others, destroying the personal property of others, lying and stealing, truancy, and a host of other socially unacceptable behaviors.

Adam exhibited defensiveness in discussing matters related to his family and his behavior at school. He declined to discuss his parents, sibling or present situation since, he said, "It is what it is, and I can do nothing about it." He stated that he got along "okay" with authority figures, but admitted he had a "bad temper." He was guarded and aloof most of the time.

Records indicate that Adam was a follower and at times found it hard to relate to his peers. He sought opportunities to do things with his peers that were destructive, such as cutting the bike tires of a neighborhood child. It was not uncommon for him to isolate himself from others, and he was often teased.

Adam was not accepted by his peer group and looked for opportunities to fight. Fighting was one of the ways the child appeared to try to dominate the group. He would even fight his female peers, a prime occasion for his male peers to make fun of him.

Adam was considered restless, inattentive, sullen, destructive, quarrelsome and disturbing of others, especially members of his peer group. It was not uncommon for Adam to be separated from his peers at both school and house outings and to require one-on-one supervision. His limited self-control, inattentiveness to directions, temper outbursts and need to "act smart," were perceived by those around him to be irresponsible and immature behavior.

The defiant, stubborn, indifferent, impudent attitude, which Adam displayed when in the company of his peers and adults outside of school, was also evident in school. The lack of effort on his part, his opposition to teachers and staff, his failure to take his studies seriously, and his immaturity when discussing key goals for the future required the child to be transferred to a three-track school, which allowed him to be placed in less academically demanding classes. Adam was not happy about the transfer, an attitude that he displayed through truancy, failure to get out of bed in the morning, and uncooperative behavior when it came to study time.

The school reported a consistent poor performance when he did attend. Adam was a destructive influence in the classroom, had poor study habits, was referred to detention often, and did homework assignments poorly if at all.

In the case record, Adam's behaviors are described through the following litany of words: "Insecure, angry, verbally demanding, likes to fight, challenging towards authority figures, feels deserted and not needed, low self-esteem, keeps others at a distance, wishes to escape, does not share his feelings, appears to struggle with being close to anyone, pulls away from peers and adults, has regressed in his present group home placement, is very impulsive, self-confidence is at an all time low, has difficulty telling the truth."

These words describe a child in a great deal of pain and suffering. The record indicates that Adam perceived his world as dehumanizing and dangerous. There is evidence of deep trauma given Adam's extensive history of multiple placements, numerous schools and caregivers, exposure to substance abuse, domestic violence, and the death of both of his parents. The lack of stability is evident in this child who is angry, depressed, and unable to make lasting connections to other human beings in his life.

Adam's multiple placement history, disruptive family experiences and acting out behavior should make him a prime candidate for mental health services. Despite these facts, he has never received a diagnostic evaluation from a trained mental health professional nor has he been referred for individual therapy as part of his overall treatment plan. And so, sadly, Adam continues down a path of personal destruction.

Mental Health Services

In reading this case study, one can have no doubt that Adam could benefit from ongoing intensive and supportive mental health services. However, the provision of these services was not a part of his overall treatment plan. Even where identified for mental health treatment, children like Adam in care are often placed on waiting lists for these services. The waiting time can be several weeks or several months, depending on the number of professional mental health workers and the provision of dollars allocated by individual states to fund services. Once assessed for treatment, children and adolescents face a managed care system in which the number of individual and group therapy sessions is limited. Mental health workers are expected to help the child or adolescent to make a speedy recovery in record time so that they can take on the next needy case. Long-term mental health therapy is not often supported, funded, nor considered a priority in treatment planning. There are just too many cases, not enough therapists and not enough funds to support ongoing mental health services for children and youth in foster care.

As anyone who has experienced a trauma will attest, the process of healing requires bonding at some level to a professional who can help a client verbalize his pain and find hope for his future. Essential to the process is the ability to recall and verbalize the journey of life at the client's own pace. For children and adolescents, making a connection to a person with the clinical skills to help them may take many sessions and require an open timeline. Most children and adolescents in care have never had the experience of bonding or attaching to an adult and may find the process new and awkward. The gathering of key information regarding the individual's family and placement history, the formation of specific insights into the needs of each child and the bonding of a trusting relationship necessitate more than one or two forty-five-minute sessions.   In addition, it is extremely important that there be continuity of therapy for the child/adolescent. Allowing more time helps the individual in treatment to remain in a stable placement for as long as mental health services are needed or at least until the individual is psychologically strong enough to return home and seek services in the local community.

Mental health services in the American foster care system are essential to the healing process of children and youth who have experienced disruption, abuse, neglect, abandonment, and serious parental dysfunction. Without access to carefully planned mental health services by professionally trained providers, children and youth in foster care are very likely to face a dismal future.

Warming the heart of a child and young adolescent in foster care through the provision of consistent, professional, and comprehensive mental health services will help to lay the foundation for a healthy and satisfying future.

Innovations Needed for Mental Health Services
Major innovations are needed in order to address the ongoing mental health needs of children and adolescents like Adam in foster care. These innovations must take into account the need for a collaborative relationship among child welfare agencies, mental health providers and mental health policymakers. In addition, attention should be given to improving linkages between child welfare agencies, professional mental health providers and mental health policy-

makers. Each of these advocacy groups must consider mental health services for children and youth in foster care as an entitlement, which is protected by law, is sustained by federal dollars, is systematically coordinated and comprehensive, and can be evaluated over time. Although states receive Social Service Block Grants as a source of funding child welfare programs, these dollars have decreased over several years (Webb & Harden, 2003). Federal dollars that are earmarked for treatment services like mental health services fall well behind those that have been allocated to support placement (Rosenbaum, 2001). Thus, children and youth coming into foster care are funded for their general housing needs but are not supported with the dollars needed to provide for an ongoing treatment plan, which should include mental health services with clear and concise clinical goals.

Providing a safe, stable and loving placement for children and youth in foster care is one very important component of the child welfare system. A stable, loving foster home, group home or residential treatment center can provide an important milieu wherein mental health professionals can begin to address mental health issues as well as the overall well-being of the child. Foster children and adolescents who find success and stability in their foster home placement are likely to feel confident enough to begin to tackle major shortcomings in their lives.

The first challenge to the child welfare agency is to find innovative ways of stabilizing the placement of behaviorally difficult foster care children and youth. Consideration should be given to the idea of live-in staff for group homes and residential treatment centers and the procurement of sufficient funds to allow for at least one foster parent to remain in the foster home full-time. A clear and concise training program for staff that have direct responsibility for handling the day-to-day activities of children and youth in care is key to the success of the placement. Providing staff with academic knowledge of how to care for marginalized children and youth, many of whom are physically, psychologically and emotionally challenging, can strengthen the underpinnings of these placements.

A second challenge to be addressed in providing for a stable placement within the child welfare agency focuses on the agency's ability to provide caseworkers. A more efficient model of frontloading intensive services to children and youth coming into foster care for the first time can help to stabilize the foster child in the initial placement and, it is hoped, provide a rapid reunification with the family where possible. The ability to frontload intensive services including mental health services requires that caseworkers assigned to each foster child have time to build relationships with their clients, assess both child and family needs promptly and make referrals to community-based agencies that provide intensive mental health services. Child welfare agencies will need to address the staffing patterns of their caseworkers and explore the need to reduce caseloads. In the long run, adequate staffing patterns, realistic caseloads, intensive services including mental health services and the stabilization of the initial foster care placement will eliminate many of the present-day challenges that both children and staff currently face in the child welfare system.

Additionally, attention must be given to the lack of available funding enabling children and youth in foster care to have access to ongoing mental health services. In reviewing admittance to mental health services for children in foster care, a key concern for child welfare personnel was the availability of community-based mental health services (Mitchell, Milner, & Hornsby, 2002). Caseworkers responsible for foster children in their care can only access mental health services that are available; thus of particular concern is accessing these ancillary community services and the funding streams that allow for their ongoing creation and future existence.

A third area of challenge concerns those responsible for mental health policy. Mental health policymakers must support the allocation of new funding from the federal government that can help to create and sustain new and innovative community- and residentially-based mental health programs. An array of mental health services, including therapeutic foster homes, community-based services, residential and day programs along with outpatient treatment centers, will help to support a more comprehensive mental health service system for children and youth in foster care and their natural families. Numerous studies have shown conclusively that intensive, community-based mental health services can be successful and financially cost-effective for children and youth with even the most severe emotional and behavioral problems (C.W.L.A, 2002). To deny or delay mental health treatment can only lead to a worsening of symptoms which may eventually require a more costly response and a higher level of residential care.

Fiscal planning with child welfare agencies must also be a part of mental health policy programming. Mental health policy planners need to assist child welfare agencies in securing funds that are available both within the child welfare system and outside of it. These various funding streams can help child welfare agencies meet the ongoing needs of children/youth and families and assist them with broad clinical support.

A fourth challenge in providing mental health services to children in foster care needs to be addressed by those who are offering mental health service, the mental health profession itself. Mental health professionals must develop and implement innovative methods of handling challenging foster-care cases. The first task should be in the form of helping child welfare agencies to access Medicaid funding in order to screen foster children for mental health problems. A nationwide survey of child welfare agencies found that agencies are funding mental health services out of their own pockets and not accessing Medicaid funding (Landsverk et al., 2001). Because Medicaid is increasingly employing managed care tactics for the provision of mental health services and other health services, child welfare agencies are finding it increasingly difficult to use Medicaid as an ongoing resource for funding mental health services (Pires, Stroul, & Armstrong, 2000). Despite this, child welfare agencies and mental health service providers need to seriously consider applying some key concepts of the managed health care system to the delivery of mental health services to child welfare. Agencies can work with managed care systems to develop diagnostic categories for children in foster care. A clear payment plan for mental health providers is essential, as is a lucid treatment plan that is open-ended until such time as the child or adolescent has reached the goal of reunification or adoption (Down, et. Al., 2004).

Mental health providers can be helpful to child welfare agencies by providing them with training in the area of meeting the mental health needs of children in foster care. Staffing personnel responsible for the daily care of children and youth in the foster care placement need to be given clear tools and methodologies for handling challenging children and adolescents with their many displays of anger and aggression. In this way, staff can gain additional insight as to why children and adolescents act out and get the education necessary to handle such challenges. Ongoing mental health training offers an opportunity to improve the overall care of foster children in the child welfare system. It presents an opportunity to enhance the well-being of the child and contributes to the general stability of the child's placement.

Mental health assessments for children and youth and their families, the diagnosis and treatment of individuals in need, and the ongoing building of a collaborative relationship with child welfare agencies, mental health professionals and mental health policymakers will help to eliminate many of the frustrations and shortcomings that children, families and professionals face in trying both to provide and to receive intensive mental health services.

In the final analysis, we need to hold those responsible for the care of our children and youth in foster care accountable for every child and adolescent in their care. This accountability must include those services foster care children are receiving on a day-to- day basis, including access to mental health evaluations, a clear treatment plan, supportive therapy by trained and licensed professionals, and the ongoing training of child welfare staff responsible for their daily lives. The healthy development of children and youth in care as well as their families must be made a high priority by child welfare agencies, mental health providers and mental health policymakers. In addition, states need to be evaluated and monitored not only on how well they are meeting the initial placement needs of foster children, but on how well they are meeting the day-to-day needs of these youngsters. An ability to provide consistent, timely and positive educational services, placement experiences and health and mental health services should be tracked and evaluated in a timely fashion.

Without these ongoing evaluations, there is no clear means of determining if the state, which is ultimately responsible for children and youth in its care, is meeting national standards. There will also be no formal means of determining if mental health services are improving for children and youth in care.

If we are to warm the stone hearts of this most vulnerable population of marginalized children and youth in our child welfare system, we need to provide the clinical support necessary for healing and wholeness. This healing and wholeness can only begin when we address the many shortcomings of the mental health system.

With child welfare agencies, mental health policymakers, state monitors and mental health professionals working together, the mental health system can be improved for children in foster care. In addressing the shortcomings of the mental health system, the improvements needed and the accountability required, children and adolescents in foster care will be offered improved access to clinical services at a time in their lives that is disruptive, turbulent and challenging, thus providing a more comprehensive and holistic approach to care.

Works Cited

Aiello, Theresa. *Child and Adolescent Treatment in Social Work Practice: A relational perspective for beginning clinicians.* New York: The Free Press, 1999.

Child Welfare Journal of Policy, Practice and Program: Special Issue: Family foster care in the next century. Retrieved May 13, 2004, from http://www.cwla.org/ programs/fostercare/jk99intr.htm.

Child Welfare League of America. Family Foster Care Fact Sheet. Retrieved May 8, 2004, from http://www.cwla.org/programs/fostercare/factsheet.htm.

Child Welfare League of America. (2003). Child Welfare Journal of Policy, Practice and Program: Special Issue: Family foster care in the next century. Retrieved June 13, 2004, from http://www.cwla.org/programs/fostercare/jf99intr.htm.

"Foster Care." *American Academy of Child and Adolescent Psychology.* 2002. Retrieved October 4, 2003, from http://www.aacap.org/publications/factsfam /64.htm.

Halfon. N., Berkowitz, G., & Klee, L. "Mental health service utilization by children in foster care in California." *Pediatrics.* 89,1992, pp. 1238-1244.

Halfon, N., Zepeda, A., Inkelas, M. "Mental health services for children in foster care." UCLA Center for Healthier Children, Families and Communities. September 2002.

Harmon, J. S., Childs, G.E., & Kelleher, K. J. "Mental health care utilization and expenditures by children in foster care." *Archives of Pediatric and Adolescent Medicine.* 154, 2000, pp. 114-1117.

Landsverk, J., Rolls, J., & the CCCW Research Team. "Preliminary results from the caring for children in child welfare project." Paper presented at the meeting of the Society for Research in Child Development, Minneapolis, April 2001.

Leslie, L. K., Hurlburt, M. S., Landsverk, J., Rolls, J. A., Wood, P.A., Kelleher, K.J. "Comprehensive assessments for children entering foster care: a national perspective." Journal of Pediatrics. July 2003.

Mitchell, L., Millner, J., & Hornsby, W. "Child and family service reviews." Paper presented at the Seventh National Child Welfare Conference, Washington, DC. March 2002.

Pires, S.A., Stroul, B. A. & Armstrong, M. I. *Health care reform tracking project: 1999 impact analysis*. Tampa: University of Florida, Louis de la Parte Florida Mental Health Institute, 2000.

Rosenbaum, B. Testimony prepared for the Human Resources Subcommittee Of the House of Representatives Committee on Ways and Means, 107th Congress (2001).

U.S. Department of Health and Human Services. "Health conditions, utilization, and expenditures of children in foster care." Washington, DC: Author. 2000.

Webb, M. B., & Harden, B. J. "Beyond child protection: promoting mental health for children and families in the child welfare system." *Journal of Emotional and Behavioral Disorders*. Spring 2003.

Chapter Six

Remembering the Children: Changing Trends in Child and Infant Death Rates and in Memorialization

Sara Ellen Kitchen

"A single death is a tragedy, a million deaths is a statistic."
Attributed to Joseph Stalin

"one death is a tragedy and a million deaths is a million tragedies, even though our imaginations may not be able to grasp that enormity. That's what the sanctity of life means." Michael N. Nagler[1]

Introduction

It is now the characteristic of a developed or industrialized nation that the death of a child is not a common or expected occurrence but a tragedy often noted in the media and memorialized by funerals, foundations, and families. But the death of a child or children is the norm for most poor families in the developing world. UNICEF reports that there are still 29,000 children under five dying daily from preventable causes. Globally, child mortality numbers have reached 10.6 million due to such causes as pneumonia, diarrhoeal diseases, malaria, measles, AIDS and malnutrition.[2] With the exception of AIDS, children have always died from these diseases. A unique dilemma is posed in developing nations. Breastfeeding is recommended to ensure the health and development of the child but it is also one of the means by which children become infected with AIDS. The moral and political challenge in the twenty-first century is that most of these child deaths are preventable. There are also some new trends to be considered in child mortality in the modern era. In the United States one of the leading causes of death for children, particularly in low-income urban areas, is gun violence. Since World War II, wars large and small have claimed children as victims and sometimes as targets. In an era that has recognized the rights of the child as integral to human rights legislation, children are not always considered as the first priority in foreign or domestic policy despite political rhetoric to the contrary. China and India are unique in demographic statistics with a higher representation of male children posing the question—what has happened to the girl children? This chapter will explore the changing trends in child mortality in the United States and the world and examine the various ways children are remembered or not in death.

History

Throughout most of human history, the deaths of infants and children remained unacknowledged and unknown. In the interdisciplinary and rapidly growing field of children's studies and the sociology of childhood, historians are now recovering and studying the documents and monuments that do attest to the death of a child. Before the nineteenth century, "the average child was the dead child."[3] European and American cemeteries of the seventeenth, eighteenth and nineteenth centuries are filled with little gravestones and tributes to the short lives of so many children. Few families raised all their children past infancy. Some of these untimely deaths are found not only by dates but also by funerary art such as the lamb on top of the stone. Some of those children have their name etched in stone. Others are referred to anonymously:

Mammy and I together lived
Just two years and a half
She went first- I followed next
The cow before the calf. *Worcester, England c.1750*
                and
The Little Hero that lies here
Was Conquered by the Diarreah. *Portland, Maine c.1800*[4]

Most families expected to lose a child in infancy and in places such as New York City one-quarter of all children born in a year were expected to die before their first birthday. Sylvia D. Hoffert notes that, for parents who performed "funereal rituals and preserving memories of their dead children . . . symptoms of grief penned in their diaries and letters are similar to those exhibited by their twentieth-century counterparts."[5] Sometimes daguerreotypes were taken of baby corpses; other parents commissioned portraits or cut off a lock of hair.[6]

Infant mortality rates among the slave population were twice that of white infants. Although considered property and potentially profitable, most slave children were subject to an early death due to poor prenatal nutrition, the poor diet after the birth, when children were denied their mother's breast more than once a day and the physical conditions in which the children were raised. Tetanus and diarrhea were two major causes of premature death.[7] Some graves in the United States are being uncovered and restored to contemporary remembrance for those children born into slavery, for the Native American children removed from tribal communities, and children institutionalized in orphanages, hospitals, and asylums. As land development occurs, construction is sometimes halted for removal of graves or historical analysis.

20th and 21st Centuries

The beginning of the twentieth century was marked in the United States and Europe by great advances in public health, sanitation reforms, medical knowledge, and education regarding the care of children. Infant death rates became the new measure of "assessing societal well-being."[8] In England in 1875 the first infant mortality rate was created, "thus suggesting for the first time a social awareness of these premature deaths and a recognition of the infant as a discrete entity"[9] among all deaths. In the United States a Children's Bureau was created in 1912 and began to measure and publish infant mortality rates in 1919. As is the case today, the United States ranked below most developed countries.[10] Although many women still breastfed their babies or relied on wet nurses, the pasteurization process of cow's milk eliminated many child deaths due to contaminated milk for the growing number of women who relied on bottle-feeding. Public health campaigns at the beginning of the 20th century to promote breastfeeding have been revived in the beginning of the 21st century. Throughout the 20th century vaccinations against the major diseases further decreased the deaths of children in the developed world. Today children must be fully immunized to attend most schools in the United States. But mandatory immunizations are not the reality or the option in many areas of the world today.

By 1910 accidents became the leading cause of death for children. Vivian Zelizer in her major book, *Pricing the Priceless Child,* relates the 1908 children's march against the New York Central Railroad. The march took place on New York City's Eleventh Avenue, otherwise known as "Death Avenue." To emphasize that so many children had lost brothers and sisters and companions to freight car killings, a child led the procession bearing the lid of a child's coffin.[11]

> It was a sad irony. Just when the campaign for the conservation of child life was making significant progress, a different death threat appeared. Railroads, streetcars, and automobiles emerged as fiercer killers of children than communicable diseases, which were rapidly being controlled by medical research and improved public health.[12]

Accidents remain one of the leading causes of death for children in the United States.

Global Child Survival and Health, a 50-year progress report published by UNICEF Canada noted that in 1955 about 210 out of every 1,000 children would die before the age of five. In 2006, estimates place 79 out of every 1,000 children dying before the age of five.[13] This downward trend truly began in 1982 when UNICEF embarked on the controversial and global program known as the Child Survival Revolution. Under the advocacy of James Grant, the Executive Director of UNICEF, and the collaboration of heads of state, non-governmental organizations (NGOs), the World Health Organization (WHO), and countless grassroots workers, national campaigns were mounted to immunize children, promote breastfeeding, and educate mothers and communities about early childhood development. It was James Grant who questioned a Salvadoran representative about low immunization rates in his country. The response that the small country was involved in a civil war prompted Jim Grant to ask," Well, why don't they stop the war so they can immunize the kids?"[14] In 1985 the first "days of tranquility" or "children's zones of peace" occurred in El Salvador where the civil war was halted for three days so that all children could be vaccinated. Since that time the "zones" have been repeated in civil wars in Uganda, Lebanon, the Sudan, and in the former Yugoslavia.[15] This decade also witnessed the drafting, ratification, and implementation of the first legally binding human rights treaty for children known as the Convention on the Rights of the Child (CRC). This human rights law was not only the most swiftly enacted human rights law in the history of the world but has been ratified by every nation in the world except the United States and Somalia (which has not had a working government). UNICEF now bases all of its work on the rights set out in the Convention and measures the progress of nations in light of its 54 articles, which stress the principles of the right to life, survival and development, non-discrimination, the best interests of the child, and respect for the views of a child.

In 1990 the World Summit for Children was held at the United Nations and, again a first for children, was attended by the largest group of world leaders ever convened for the purpose of reducing infant and child mortality among other human development goals. In 2000 the member states of the United Nations reaffirmed their commitment to the children of the world with the Millennium Development Goals to be met by 2015. At an international conference in London in December 2005, UNICEF's Executive Director Ann M. Veneman said, "Child mortality is one of the world's most urgent crises—and one of the most preventable. By seizing the opportunity to reach this Millennium Development Goal [number 4: reduce child mortality], we could save 30 million young lives in the decade ahead, 10 million through immunization alone."[16]

The eradication of smallpox due to worldwide immunization has been one of the public health success stories of the twentieth century (although the World Health Organization declared the world free of smallpox in 1980 the storage of the virus in laboratories in the United States and Russia poses a future threat for germ warfare)[17] The eradication of polio is near. Through the Child Survival Campaign more than 70 % of the world's children became immunized against diphtheria, whooping cough, tetanus, polio, and measles in the 1980s. But, while these rates have decreased in some nations, they have remained uneven in others[18]

Although there has been continued overall progress in lowering infant mortality rates in the past decade, a recent UNICEF report points out that in some nations, particularly in sub-Saharan Africa, rates of child mortality have increased due to the HIV/AIDS epidemic[19] and economic conditions. *The Sunday Times of London* reported on April 2, 2006 that officials were finding at least 20 corpses of newborn babies each week in the drains of Zimbabwe's capital, Harare. Pediatricians anonymously interviewed by reporters said, "severe child malnutrition had doubled over the past year and hospital morgues were piled high with bodies people could not afford to bury."[20] In Botswana, a country with the second highest incidence of HIV/AIDS infected mothers, the AIDS-related death of babies has increased by 20%. A UNICEF country report states that inscriptions on tombstones are a "stark warning: Born 2004. Died 2004."[21] Infants born to HIV/AIDS infected mothers are infected, through birth or breastfeeding, at the rate of 2,000 a day according to UNICEF. Most of these infants will die before their fifth birthday.[22]

> For HIV-positive mothers with limited access to clean water and sanitation, the choice of whether to breastfeed or not can be a painful dilemma. New mothers must weigh the risk of passing on the infection to their infants against the risk of denying them breast milk. During the first two months, a bottle-fed baby is nearly six times more likely to die from diarrhoeal, respiratory or other infections, compared to a breastfed child, mostly because contaminated water is used in mixing the formula, bottles are unclean and other reasons.[23]

UNICEF, WHO, and other NGOs in the field try to provide education, antiretroviral drugs, and other health initiatives but drugs are expensive and national economic, environmental or political factors make the challenge of saving children's lives due to HIV/AIDS particularly difficult and a block to achieving MDG goals. In October of 2005, a new global campaign was launched to put a child's face on the AIDS epidemic with UNICEF and UNAIDS joining as UNITE FOR CHILDREN, UNITE AGAINST AIDS.[24]

Lancet, the leading international medical journal, published a series of articles in 2003 on child survival. The great strides made by UNICEF and others in reducing infant child mortality were noted with an emphasis on the three actions that were critical to continued decline—exclusive breastfeeding for the first six months, the use of bed nets to protect children from contracting malaria, and the use of oral rehydration salts to combat diarrhea.[25]

Children in War

It is often said that all wars are wars against children. This past century and the first years of the 21st century have witnessed the deaths of millions of children. It is estimated that one and a half million children were killed in the Holocaust.[26] Other children died from the bombs and starvation associated with World War II in Europe and Asia where civilians were particularly targeted by military actions. UNICEF (the original name referred to the International Children's Emergency Fund, or ICEF) was created as a temporary organization for emergency relief for children in post-war Europe. Only with the outcry from a

Pakistan delegate at the United Nations General Assembly in 1950 that children in the developing world were suffering not from post-war conditions but from age-old poverty did UNICEF become a permanent organization in1953 and the International ('I') and the Emergency ('E') were formally dropped from the title.[27] Violence against children by war did not end with World War II. On a large scale, children were victims in the Vietnam War during the 1960s and 1970s. Who can forget the image of the child fleeing down a road naked and with burns from napalm? That child did survive until adulthood but thousands more children lost their lives in the "killing fields" of Cambodia, the wars in Central America, the civil wars in Myanmar (Burma), Sudan, Rwanda, Uganda, Congo and the former Yugoslavia. "It is estimated—and estimates are all that can be offered- that 150 million children have been killed in war and civil war since the 1970s, around the world. . . . It was as if every North American child born in the same period had been killed or injured."[28] UNICEF and other relief and human rights organizations have been involved with bringing to light the plight of children during these wars, as part of the wars, and in the aftermath of war. The vast majority of fatalities related to all these conflicts are women and children.[29]

During the recent wars in Iraq, the Gulf War of 1990, and the present war in 2006, hundreds of thousands of children have died due to war violence, starvation and disease related to embargos and destruction of the health infrastructure.[30] In Northern Uganda, Olara Ottunu, former Under Secretary General for Children in Armed Conflict, claims that it is the worst place on earth to be a child in 2006. Children have become "night commuters" traveling several hours each night to sleep in town streets to avoid abduction by the infamous Lord's Resistance Army or living in concentration camps that have the worst infant mortality rates in the world. The United Nations has confirmed that the death rates in the camps in Uganda of over 1,000 children a week are double those of the Darfur region in the Sudan.[31]

One of the major concerns of the United Nations and UNICEF has been the use and abuse of child soldiers in many of parts of the war-torn world. Child soldiers have always been part of recorded war history. Children were part of the American revolutionary forces.[32] This author's great-grandfather lied about his age to fight in the Civil War.[33] What is different today is that there has been a nearly universally ratified treaty prohibiting the conscription of youth under the age of 18.[34] The United Nations has even created a special office and position of Under-Secretary General for Children in Armed Conflict in response to the commissioned 1996 Report on the Impact of Armed Conflict on Children presented to the United Nations General Assembly by Graca Machel.[35] Modern child soldiers first came to the attention of the world during the Iran-Iraq war, "when half a million Iranian boys aged between 12 and 18 were recruited into the armed forces and thousands were reported to have lost their lives functioning as human mine detectors."[36]

In the aftermath of war, landmines are often the ongoing killers of children. UNICEF estimates that 30%-40% of the yearly 15,000 to 20,000 people killed or maimed by landmines are younger than 15. Children are often killed instantly or before they reach a hospital. UNICEF and the International Campaign to Ban Landmines are engaged in efforts not only to demine 82 mine-affected countries around the world but also to educate children who are attracted to the landmines as curious playthings.[37]

Children have also been specific targets in recent wars to torture parents or demoralize a society. In the "Dirty War" of thirty years ago in Argentina thousands of children and grandchildren were "lost" or "disappeared" as part of the military's campaign to halt any political dissidence. Brave mothers made history as the *Madres of the Plaza de Mayo and Abuelas of the Plaza de Mayo* as they marched in front of the presidential palace in Buenos Aires every week for decades demanding justice and information about their children and the grandchildren born in captivity. The *Abuelas* are now credited not only with proposing the Article 8 in the Convention on the Rights of the Child—"States Parties undertake to respect the right of a child to preserve his or her identity, including nationality, name and family relations as recognized by law without unlawful interference."—but also with expanding forensic science to include the first genetic data bank so that the children born in prison and illegally adopted by military members can discover their identity at a future date. "To date, the *Abuelas* have located and identified ninety-seven of the 'living disappeared.'"[38] Their children and grandchildren will not be forgotten.

Invisible Children in Life and Death

The State of the World's Children 2006 the annual report published by UNICEF has a special focus on invisible and vulnerable children.[39] Article 7 of the Convention on the Rights of the Child (CRC) emphasizes that birth registration is a fundamental human right: "The child shall be registered immediately after birth and shall have the right from birth to a name."[40] In 2003 UNICEF reported that 48 million children or 36% of total births went unregistered. In sub-Saharan Africa the percentage rose to 62% and in South Asia to 70%. Without legal recognition, children may be denied important health and human services, may be at risk for abduction and conscription into armed forces, and may never be acknowledged in death as a person or as a statistic. Most unregistered births are the children of poor families who live too far from government offices, live as refugees, live in war-torn areas, or are daily struggling to survive. [41]

In her acclaimed anthropological study, *Death Without Weeping,* Nancy Scheper-Hughes recounts the reality of women in Northeast Brazil who do not register their children nor even name them at birth due to high infant mortality rates. A poor woman may keep statistics in her head and when asked how many children she has in her family, "she invariably replies with the formula, 'X children, y living.' Sometimes she may say, 'Y living, z angels.'"[42] Scheper-Hughes discovered in her research that official statistics were unreliable and understated for infant deaths. Due to cultural customs, unbaptized children were not registered until the late 1980s because they were "stigmatized" by parents and buried "covertly."[43] Often baptisms were delayed for up to a year to see if a child would live. Another reason for non-registration was due the fact that many children were born at home with the assistance of midwives who were practicing outside official medical regulations. Scheper- Hughes attempted to get a more accurate account of infant deaths by interviewing the local coffin maker who made cardboard coffins for children at the request of the local municipality. When she asked why his records did not reflect data on baby coffins, "he replied, 'Because it wouldn't be of interest to anyone.' The deaths of these children, like their brief lives, are invisible and of little or no account."[44] Although birth registration is mandatory, Scheper-Hughes notes that most families do not register their children until they must confront the "state", usually for primary school registration.[45] Although her research is confined to one community in Northeast Brazil, Bom de Jesus da Mata, Scheper-Hughes relates the reality for so many of the world's poor families living in "an environment where death is understood as the most ordinary and most expected outcome for the children. . . ."[46]

Girl Children

One of the unusual demographic realities of the late twentieth and early twenty-first centuries is that more boy babies are born and live in India and China contrary to normal demographic statistics. There are cultural explanations for this phenomenon. In China the one child per family policy instituted in 1979 to limit population growth has resulted in the preferred child being male. For centuries it has been the Asian tradition for a son to care for the parents when they grow old. Girls traditionally joined the household of the husband's family and cared for his parents. Until the easing of the policy in some rural areas in 1984 to allow for a second child if the first child was a girl,[47] families often neglected, malnourished, abandoned, or sometimes even killed the girl infant. In India, male children are also preferred over girls who are seen as a financial burden on families due to dowry customs. In rural areas, girl children may not be registered at birth and may be neglected until an early death. *The Lancet* series questions the accuracy of death registration and cause of death registration statistics in India and China.[48] In urban areas, girl children's lives were terminated before birth through abortion after sex determination. In 1996 India banned the use of ultrasound technology for such purposes although the practice continues illegally.[49] All of these girl children are made invisible by death.

Poor and Abandoned Children

Pauper's graves and potter's fields are terms reminiscent of a bygone era in Europe and the United States. It was considered a social stigma to be buried as a pauper. As infant mortality rates decreased in the United States in the early 1900s, the new phenomena of child life insurance policies emerged in the working and middle classes to avoid the "degradation" of a pauper burial. Child insurance payments often took precedence in the family budget reflecting the "sacralization" of the child. Jacob Riis and others were critical of this business, claiming it prompted parents to neglect children for the insurance proceeds and the child saving organizations of the day fought many battles in state legislatures and in the press to attempt to halt the profitable business of child insurance policies.[50] "The sentimentalization of childhood cut across social class distinctions; the sacred child was mourned with new intensity even in the poorest homes."[51] Providing a memorial stone with a loving inscription for a deceased child had now become the cultural norm.

Today communities still set ground aside for burial of the indigent and assume the cost of burying or cremating the poor and abandoned. In 1990 the *New York Times* reported on the burial by correctional inmates of 1,606 poor babies on Hart Island noting that indigent infants were buried more often than poor adults in this largest of New York City's cemeteries, a potter's field since 1869. In fact, almost half of all children in the past decade born below the poverty level and dying before the age of one were buried on Hart Island. "A Catholic priest sometimes comes to bless God's little children, en masse. A crumbling monument donated by a tombstone company squats by a derelict road. 'Cry not for us,' it says.' We are at peace.'"[52] In Calimesa, California, east of Los Angeles, another anonymous burial site holds the graves of over 40 infants picked up at various coroners' offices by a woman intent on honoring these children in death. Only the date of burial is noted, not names, or dates of birth or death.[53] One non-profit organization on Long Island was founded by emergency medical technicians in response to such cases of abandonment and buries children with dignified funerals.[54]

Another acknowledgement that infants are still abandoned in America has been the passage of safe-haven laws or Baby Moses legislation by most states. In 1999 Texas was the first state to pass such legislation in response to the discovery of 13 abandoned babies in Houston in a ten-month period. Statistics are not accurate but estimates indicate that more than 20,000 infants are abandoned yearly with almost 7,000 found dead.[55] The purpose of the safe haven laws is to encourage mothers or others to drop-off unwanted infants at a designated spot such as a hospital, church or police or fire station and receive immunity from any criminal prosecution. The state laws vary in designating specific drop-off locations and the age of the infant. If they don't take advantage of these laws, parents or guardians may be charged with neglect or abandonment.[56] Critics of these laws claim that little is done to address the "social and economic pressures that cause a parent to abandon a newborn baby"[57]

In Romania, Russia, and China, Human Rights Watch has documented thousands of children left to die in orphanages and institutions for the disabled and abandoned.[58] Their existence and death remains a tenuous statistic.

Poverty is directly or indirectly related to most child deaths. Poverty in the developing world contributes to the existence of the millions of street children in urban areas. Early deaths are linked to violence, drugs, AIDS, and lack of health care. The situation of street children in Brazil has been well-documented and studied. In 1989 one study found that 457 children were murdered or "executed" on the streets of Rio, Sao Paulo, and Recife. Most of these children were young males who had known addresses and living parents.

These crimes, which resembled executions, are believed to have been committed by hired gunmen. Police are investigating drug traffickers and gangsters who are the prime suspects; individuals who take justice into their own hands ("vigilantes", "death or extermination squads"); and a third group, the, the military and civil police and private security guards. Few of these cases have been resolved. It is worth emphasizing that the victims are commonly perceived as *a social evil which should be suppressed [italics added].*[59]

The attention of the world press has resulted in legislation and human service responses to this national tragedy and renewed attention to the lives of street children everywhere. In addition to UNICEF and other NGOs working with children, the street children of the world have organized nationally and internationally.

The United States is by no means immune from violence against children in the street or the home. A recent study of homicide rates in the United state considers guns as one factor in the rising homicide rates of children. The Office of Juvenile Justice and Delinquency Prevention (OJDDP) states that homicide is the only major cause of childhood deaths that has increased over the past three decades.[60] "What can be said with confidence is that there has been a worsening of the U.S. child homicide situation. . . ."[61] The Children's Defense Fund (CDF) reports that the number of children and teens killed by gun violence alone in 2003 exceeded the number of American military killed in hostile action in Iraq from 2003 to April 2006. Most of these deaths were boys and minorities. The rate of firearm deaths among children under age 15 is higher in the United States than in 25 other industrialized nations combined. "Since 1993, when CDF launched its campaign to protect children against gun violence, the death rate of children and youth by gunfire has declined from almost 16 a day to just under 8 a day. This is still a morally obscene statistic for the world's most powerful country, which has more resources to address its social ills than any other nation."[62] The easy availability of guns is one major cause of these statistics, according to Dr. Edward Cornwell, Professor of Surgery and Chief of Adult Trauma at John Hopkins University but so "is popular culture that condones underachievement and glamorizes brutality."[63] He recalls stitching up a teen with 15 stab wounds and "Kill or Be Killed"[64] tattooed across his chest.

Children's Memorials and Commemoration

How children are remembered or not in death reflects their social status in a community and their "marginalization" in society.[65] Memorializing children in the past and present centuries has taken many different forms.

Three significant commemorations in stone since World War II are worth mentioning. At Yad Vashem, the Holocaust Memorial in Israel one of the more impressive monuments is the Children's Memorial in which the light of memorial candles is reflected by mirrors inside a cave to remember the 1.5 million children who perished in the Holocaust. In Hiroshima's Peace Park the statue of Sadako (also known as The Children's Monument) is surrounded by millions of paper cranes often made by children from around the world as a symbol of hope and peace that no nuclear war will again destroy human life. Another statue of hope is at the University for Peace in Costa Rica; it depicts a mother holding an infant with the inscription in Spanish translated as "Happy the Costa Rican mother who when she gives birth to a son knows that he will never be a soldier." Costa Rica abolished their military forces in 1948.

The Day of the African Child is celebrated on June 16 to commemorate that day in 1976 when thousands of black children in South Africa took to the streets in Soweto to protest their inferior education. Hundred of children were shot and killed. This day has been observed since 1991 when the Organization of African Unity first initiated it. In 2006 the theme was "Violence Against Children," an ongoing concern in Africa and elsewhere.[66]

Children commemorating children is not a new phenomenon. In the late 1800s and early 1900s newsboy funerals made the news. To avoid the shame and anonymity of paupers' graves, young newsboys collected from their peers to offer flowers, hearses, undertakers, and ministers to remember their friends in the manner which the custom of the day afforded the middle classes. One such example was the case of John Ellard in Philadelphia, also known as Didley Dumps. His biography and burial were published in the *American Sunday School Union*. "He was given a 'grand ' funeral that included a cortege of fifty-six newsboys, six of whom carried his body from the home on Pear Street to St. Joseph's Church. At sixth and Chestnut they passed Ellard's newsstand, which had been draped in black crepe and tied with white ribbon, 'indicating that the adornment was for one of tender years.'"[67] These funerals and burials provided newsboys with an identity that signified "that they were not just vagrants and beggars, but members of a trade, and not just anonymous hawkers, but individuals who had names. . . . Only through ritual could the death of one enhance the status of all."[68]

Children in New York City paraded up Fifth Avenue to Central Park on October 9, 1922, to a Child Memorial erected in honor of accident victims. "According to press reports, 'all eyes were turned,' to a special division of 1,054 boys representing an equal number of children accidentally killed during 1921."[69] Other child mourning tributes were organized by the Boy Scouts and Girl Scouts each Saturday to remember the victims of accidents. Public safety programs became a national and local response to these "group mourning" events.[70]

A contemporary cultural reflection of the death of a child in urban America is the T-shirt memorial. "The shirts are a uniquely modern twist on the ancient ritual of honoring the dead, springing from today's turbulent inner-city street culture and cheap computer technology that enables entrepreneurs to charge about $16 a throw for what amount to wearable tombstones."[71] Shirts are worn to funerals and wakes, on the anniversary of deaths, on birthdays of the deceased, and as an everyday fashion particularly among gang members. Another symbol to memorialize a death is the decals on car windows. "They don't have to be stonemasons," Jack Jensen of the California Funeral Directors Association says, "They're going to act out their expression in a medium that they're quite adept at working with."[72] Although impermanent, such memorials are creative, can be mass-produced and generate a sense of solidarity among the grieving. Other urban memorials are referred to in the press as "makeshift memorials" or by scholars of popular culture as "spontaneous shrines."[73] Where a child has been gunned down, a street shrine or altar may arise as people place pictures, stuffed animals, notes, candles, and other mementos to recognize the dead child or youth. *The Philadelphia Inquirer* has an occasional series chronicling the gun deaths of local teens in photos, slide shows, and reports. The slideshow on "Mook", age 15, shot in South Philadelphia on January 14, 2006, notes his name was "spray painted on abandoned houses, tattooed on friends' forearms, scrawled on teddy bears on the sidewalk . . . where he was killed."[74] The cyber-shrine or webpage is yet another contemporary means of memorializing the deaths of children and youth. One study analyzing the memorials posted on the Virtual Memorial Garden (VMG) notes that children posted at least one-third of all memorials and the postings often took the form of letters to the deceased. Religious references were limited in these web cemeteries, perhaps reflecting the nature of cyberspace communities, but the grief expressed by parents conveys the same emotional pain as the diaries of an earlier century.[75] "It is so taboo to talk about a dead child," remarked one mother who made memorials on Legacy.com and Memory-of-.com for her four-year-old daughter who died in March 2005, "That's one thing the Internet has [changed]. In the past, if you were to walk into a grocery store, you wouldn't know you weren't the only person who had lost a child."[76] Children themselves utilize such social networking websites as MySpace.com to memorialize their friends.

Conclusion

The deaths of so many children in the United States and the world are preventable. Laws regarding gun ownership and manufacturing can be changed. National and global policies regarding poverty, health, the environment, and military spending may be similarly responsive to civil society's care and concern for others. Americans are caught up in a "death culture," according to Jeremy Rifkin, in their pursuit of the American dream at all costs. We "reward the powerful and marginalize the vulnerable" through excessive consumption of material goods, environmental resources and energy, and military might.[77] Policies and practices are not etched in stone nor should the hearts of the non-marginalized world citizens be impervious to world suffering and death.

In his address to the Eighth International Vatican Conference in 1993, the late James Grant, then Executive Director of UNICEF, stated:

I would argue that no features of contemporary global reality better illustrates the central human dilemma of our times than the deaths, year in and year out, of some 13 million children under the age of five. Each one of them has the same right to live, each has the same right to fulfill his or her potential, each has the same right to be loved and cared for, each has the same right to contribute to civilization, as the child of the wealthiest and most privileged of families. For most of human history, such deaths were largely inevitable; but now we know how to prevent or cure the diarrhoea, the pneumonia, and the measles that account for most of these deaths, not only in prosperous homes but also in the world's most remote, impoverished villages, what was once tragic but largely unavoidable has become morally unconscionable—an obscenity— today. Given this welcome change—our greatly enhanced capacity to prevent child death and disability—we must ask ourselves why do so many continue to tolerate this massive needless loss of life? Should not morality march with increasing capacity?[78]

In *Soul of a Citizen,* Paul Rogat Loeb challenges the hearts of minds of Americans. "Too often, we're taught to ignore or excuse the pain inflicted on the distant and not-so-distant children of others. To be sure, we'll always listen most attentively to our own children's cries. But if, we don't heed the cries of others' as well, American will be lost, and we'll risk losing our souls."[79] Since James Grant spoke to the Vatican in 1993, overall statistics have improved for child mortality. Still in 2006 UNICEF counts 11 million child deaths a year—30,000 a day—of children under the age of five dying due to preventable causes. In the world's poorest countries, some child mortality rates have actually increased.[80]

This chapter has attempted to remember the children both living and dead. There are many children whose story has not been told or documented in life and death. This chapter, however, has not attempted to be exhaustive but is meant to encourage further research, advocacy, and action on behalf of all our children. As James Grant insisted and as Jeffrey Sachs, in *The End of Poverty,*[81] has most recently reminded us, extreme poverty in the world can be eliminated with the modest help of the rich nations. It is within our economic capacity as a global society. The efforts of Bill and Melinda Gates are to be applauded and replicated, but it will take many partnerships and commitments by nations, organizations, and citizens. Legal scholars may claim that all rights are equal but some rights and people are entitled to priority for without that recognition all human rights are betrayed. Jim Grant once asked a little Ethiopian girl what she wanted to be when she grew up. "Alive" she responded.[82] Child survival and development is such a priority. Children need most to be remembered in life so as to not be remembered as children in death.

Notes

1. Michael N. Nagler, *Is there No Other Way? The Search for a Nonviolent Future* (Berkeley, CA: Berkeley Hills Books, 2001), p. 287.

2. www.unicef.org (2006).

3. Judith Sealander, *The Failed Century of the Child. Governing America's Young in the Twentieth Centur.* (New York, NY: The Cambridge University Press, 2003). p. 7.

4. E. R. Shushan, *Grave Matter.* (New York: Ballantine Books, 1990.), p. 144.

5. Sylvia D. Hoffert, " 'A Very Peculiar Sorrow': Attitudes Toward Infant Death in the Urban Northeast, 1800-1860,"*American Quarterly* 39: 4 (1987), p. 601.

6. Hoffert, p. 602.

7. Steven Mintz, *Huck's Raft. A History of American Childhood* (Cambridge, MA: The Belknap Press, 2004). pp. 96-97.

8. Jacqueline H. Wolf, *Don't Kill Your Baby. Public Health and the Decline of Breastfeeding in the 19th and 20th Centuries* (Columbus, Ohio: The Ohio State University Press, 2001), p. 45.

9. Nancy Scheper-Hughes, *Death Without Weeping. The Violence of Everyday Life in Brazi.* (Berkley, CA: University of California Press, 1992), p. 274.

10. Wolf, p. 226.

11. Viviana A. Zelizer, *Pricing the Priceless Child. The Changing Social Value of Children* (New York, NY: Basic Books, 1985), p. 32.

12. Zelizer. p. 32-33.

13. *Global Child Survival and Health.* UNICEF Canada (2006).

14. *Jim Grant. UNICEF Visionary.* (Florence, Italy: UNICEF Innocenti Research Centre, 2000), p. 28.

15. Maggie Black, *Children First: The story of UNICEF, Past and Present* (New York, NY: Oxford University Press, 1996). p. 46.

16. www.unicef.org (2006).

17. Sealander, p. 352.

18. www.unicef.org (2006).

19. Ibid.

20. Christine Lamb, "Desperate Mothers Throw Away 20 Babies a Week as Zimbabwe Starves," *The Sunday Times.* (London, England: April 2, 2006), p. 20.

21. www.unicef.org/infobycountry/botswana.

22. www.unicef.org (2006).

23. Ibid.

24. Ibid.

25. Robert E. Black, Saul S. Morris, and Jennifer Bryce, "Where and Why are 10 Million Children Dying Every Year?" *The Lancet* 361:2226-34 (2003).

26. Peter N. Stearns, *Childhood in World History* (New York, NY: Routledge, 2006), p.110.

27. Black, p. 8.

28. Stearns, p. 112.

29. Ibid.

30. Ibid.

31. Olara A. Ottunnu, "Death of a People," *Christian Century.* 123:8 (2006), p. 11-12.

32. Stearns, p. 115.

33. Richard Gibney enlisted at age 15 to fight with Union soldiers. He shook Abraham Lincoln's hand when he was 17 and then of legal age.

34. Optional Protocol on the Involvement of Children in Armed Conflict. www.unhchr.ch/html/menu2/6/protocol.htm.

35. Graca Machel, *The Impact of War on Childre.* (London, UK: Hurst & Company, 2001).

36. Black. p. 259.

37. www.unicef.org. *Children and Landmines: A Deadly Legacy.* (2006)

38. Lisa Avery, "A Return to Life: The Right to Identity and the Right To Identify Argentina's 'Living Disappeared,'"*Harvard Women's Law Journal* 27:270 (2004).

39. *The State of the World's Children 2006* is the latest in series of annual publications that is the most comprehensive survey of global trends affecting children and provides the most accurate statistics available. Governments, NGOS, and academic institutions use it.   Statistics are available at www.unicef.org/sow06/statistics/statistics.php.

40. United Nations Convention on the Rights of the Child (1989).

41. *State of the World's Children 2006.* UNICEF.

42. Nancy Scheper-Hughes, *Death Without Weeping. The Violence of Everyday Life in Brazil* (Berkeley, California: The University of California Press, 1992), p. 286.

43. Scheper-Hughes, p. 291.

44. Ibid.

45. Scheper-Hughes, p. 292.

46. Scheper-Hughes, p. 20.

47. Racheal Savanyu, "International Watch: The Public Womb Under China's One-Child Policy" 9 Buff. *Women's L.J.* 18 (2000).

48. *Lancet.* p. 2229.

49. Interview with Carol Bellamy, Executive Director, UNICEF. *The Georgetown Public Policy Review* 9 (2003), p. 25.

50. For more background on the controversy of child insurance see Chapter 4, "From a Proper Burial to a Proper Education: The Case of Children's Insurance," in Viviana Selizer, *Pricing the Priceless Child.*

51. Zelizer, p. 131.

52. Douglas Martin, "About New York: A Heavy Burden: Burying Eileen, Sam, Liz and F/C," *The New York Times* (March 28, 1990).

53. "Garden of Angels," www.pbs.org/newhour/essays, April 7, 2000.

54. " www.amtchildrenofhope.com/profile.

55. Susan L. Pollet, "Safe-Haven Laws-Do Legal Havens to Abandon Babies Save Lives?" *Westchester Bar Journal* 32:71 (2005).

56. Pollet, p. 72.

57. Debbe Magnusen, "From Dumpster to Delivery Room: Does Legalizing Baby Abandonment Really Solve the Problem?" *Juvenile Justice Law Journal* 22: 21 (2001/2002).

58. www.hrw.org./children/abandoned (2006).

59. Rizzini, quoted in William A. Corsaro, *The Sociology of Childhood 2nd. Ed.* (Thousand Oaks, CA: Pine Forge Press, 2005), p. 254.

60. OJJDP *Juvenile Justice Bulletin,* October 2001.

61. Colin Pritchard and Alan Butler, "A Comparative Study of Children and Adult Homicide Rates in the USA and the Major Western Countries 1974-1999: Grounds for Concern," *Journal of Family Violence.* 18:6 (2003), p. 341.

62. Children's Defense Fund. 2006, www.childrensdefense.org.

63. Ibid.

64. Ibid.

65. Corsaro, p. 6.

66. www.unicefusa.org (2006).

67. Vincent DiGirolamo. "Newsboy Funerals: Tales of Sorrow and Solidarity in Urban America," *Journal of Social History.*36: 1 (2002), p. 13.

68. DiGirolamo, p. 26

69. Zelizer, p. 41.

70. Zelizer, p. 43.

71. Dan Morse, "Fraught Couture: Shirts for the Dead Are the New Rage In Some Inner Cities--- They Memorialize Victims of Violence; Do They Glorify the Thug Life? —'More T-shirts Than Friends'" *The Wall Street Journal.* (Feb. 4, 1999), p. A1.

72. Kate Moser, "New Memorials: t-shirts, websites, auto decals," *Christian Science Monitor* (May 25, 2006).

73. Sylvia Gride,. "Spontaneous Shrines: A Modern Response to Tragedy and Disaster," *New Directions in Folklore.* 5 (2001).

74. http://www.philly.com/mld/inquirer/news/special-packages/gunviolence (2006).

75. Brian deVries and Judy Rutherford, "Memorializing Loved Ones on the World Wide Web" *Omega.* 49 (2004), pp. 5-26.

76. Moser, "New Memorials."

77. Jeremy Rifkin, *The European Dream* (New York, NY: Penguin Group, 2004), p. 379.

78. Jim Grant, in *Jim Grant,* p. 168.

79. Paul Rogat Loeb, *Soul of a Citizen. Living with Conviction in a Cynical Time* (New York: St. Martin's Griffin, 1999), p. 184.

80. www.unicef.org (2006).

81 Jeffrey Sachs, *The End of Poverty: Economic Possibilities for Our Time* (.New York, NY: Penguin Press, 2005).

82. *Jim Grant,* p. 156.

Works Cited

Avery, Lisa. "A Return to Life: The Right to Identity and the Right to Identify Argentina's 'Living Disappeared.'" *Harvard Women's Law Journal* 27:270 (2004).

Black, Maggie. *Children First: The Story of UNICEF, Past and Present.* New York: Oxford University Press, 1996.

Black, Robert E., Saul S. Morris, and Jennifer Bryce. "Where and Why Are 10 Million Children Dying Every Year?" *The Lancet* 361 (2003): pp. 2226-2234.

Corsaro, William A. *The Sociology of Children 2nd Edition.* Thousand Oaks, CA: Pine Forge Press, 2005.

DeVries, Brian and Judy Rutherford. "Memorializing Loved Ones on the World Wide Web." *Omega* 49 (2004).

DiGirolamo, Vincent. "Newsboy Funerals: Tales of Sorrow and Solidarity in Urban America." *Journal of Social History* 36:1 (2002).

Grider, Sylvia. "Spontaneous Shrines: A Modern Response to Tragedy and Disaster." *New Directions in Folklore* 5 (2001).

Hoffert, Sylvia D. "'A Very Peculiar Sorrow:' Attitudes Toward Infant Death in the Urban Northeast, 1800-1860." *American Quarterly* 39: 4 (1987).

Lamb, Christine. "Desperate Mothers Throw Away 20 Babies a Week as Zimbabwe Starves." *The Sunday Times.* London, April 2, 2006.

Loeb, Paul Rogat. *Soul of a Citizen: Living with Conviction in a Cynical Time.* New York: St. Martin's Griffin, 1999.

Machel, Graca. *The Impact of War on Children.* London: Hurst & Company, 2001.

Magnusen, Debbe. "From Dumpster to Delivery Room: Does Legalizing Baby Abandonment Really Solve the Problem?" *Juvenile Justice Law Journal* 22:21 (2001/2002).

Martin, Douglas. "About New York: A Heavy Burden: Burying Eileen, Sam, Liz and F/C." *The New York Times* (March 28, 1990).

Mintz, Steven. *Huck's Raft: A History of American Childhood.* Cambridge, MA: The Belknap Press, 2004.

Morse, Dan. "Fraught Couture: Shirts for the Dead Are the New Rage in Some Inner Cities—They Memorialize Victims of Violence: Do They Glorify the Thug Life?—More T-shirts than Friends." *The Wall Street Journal* (February 4, 1999).

Moser, Kate. "New Memorials: t-shirts, websites, auto decals." *The Christian Science Monitor* (May 25, 2006).

Nagler, Michael N. *Is There No Other Way? The Search for a Nonviolent Future.* Berkeley, CA: Berkeley Hills Books, 2001.

Ottunnu, Olara A. "Death of a People." *The Christian Century* 123:8 (2006), pp. 11-12.

Pollet, Susan L. "Safe-Haven Laws—Do Legal Havens to Abandon Babies Save Lives?" *Westchester Bar Journal* 32:71 (2005).

Pritchard, Colin and Alan Butler. "A Comparative Study of Children and Adult Homicide Rates in the USA and the Major Western Countries 1974-1999: Grounds for Concern." *Journal of Family Violence* 18:6 (2002).

Sachs, Jeffrey. *The End of Poverty: Economic Possibilities for Our Time.* New York: Penguin Press, 2005.

Savanyu, Rachel. "International Watch: The Public Womb Under China's One-Child Policy." *Women's Law Journal* 18 (2000).

Scheper-Hughes, Nancy. *Death without Weeping: The Violence of Everyday Life in Brazil.* Berkeley, CA: University of California Press, 1992.

Sealander, Judith. *The Failed Century of the Child: Governing America's Young in the Twentieth Century.* New York: Cambridge University Press, 2003.

Shushan, E. R. *Grave Matters.* New York: Ballantine Books, 1990.

Stearns, Peter N. *Childhood in World History.* New York: Routledge, 2006.

Wolf, Jacqueline H. *Don't Kill Your Baby. Public Health and the Decline of Breastfeeding in the 19th and 20th Centuries.* Columbus, OH: Ohio State University Press, 2001.
Zelizer, Viviana A. *Pricing the Priceless Child: The Changing Social Value of Children.* New York: Basic Books, 1985.

Chapter Seven

As Unyielding as Stone:
Group Behavior and the Question of War

Nancy L. Porter

"Madness is the exception in individuals but the rule in groups."
Nietzsche

The dynamics of group behavior that are associated with warfare encompass forces that range from evolutionary biology to the social sciences. As a species with no known predators, and with unmatched cognitive and communicative capacity in the animal world, the human's persistent connection with warfare against its own kind endures. Illogical in terms of its consistent failure to deliver desired results yet relentless in its tie to human affairs, the interrelations of the social and biological origins of this core human tendency are complex, conjectural, yet critically important in addressing the circumstances around a specific sort of intraspecies conflict unknown in the animal world.

Sociobiology has argued that war is the form of natural selection that a species without predators has developed in a society of competitive cultures. (Doyle, 1997) The inherent aggressive and protective tendencies noted in other species make logical sense in the thesis that competition and aggression are natural, evolved human traits. (Barash, 1994, Doyle, 1997) Research in psychology has affirmed the cross-cultural ethnocentric tendencies of all humans and the psychic ease with which they create out groups or enemies within this context. (Sherif & Sherif, 1979, Tajfel & Turner, 1979) In contrast, sociology and anthropology have largely rejected the automatic nature of human aggression in warfare, instead suggesting that war is an unfortunate and regrettable accident or choice of which society has the innate ability to rid itself. (Doyle, 1997, Mead, 2000). The interlocking of evolution and instinct theory, brain development, language, the psyche, and the power of culture to influence behavior provide the complex terrain on which the roots of human warfare subsist.

There is a paradoxical dimension of connecting warfare to Darwinian notions or sociobiology as this theory has much to do with the individual struggle for survival and seems antithetical to the notion that war requires and produces the sacrifice of individuals, often the "fittest" of the species, for the welfare of the group. If war is a form of group selection, then altruism, or the tendency to sacrifice for the group must have some sort of adaptive advantage. (Doyle, 1997) Group living and cooperativeness proved beneficial to early humans as they allowed for improved detection of predators or enemies, cooperation in hunting and gathering food and in caring for offspring, and safe places for sleeping and breeding. The down side of communal living was seen in conflicts of interest regarding limited resources such as sexual partners, increased risk of disease, and greater risk of parental exploitation or infanticide/cannibalism by other group members. (van der Dennen, 1995). The most successful early groups logically, then, were those with maximum cooperation within, those in which the group promoted and perhaps enforced cooperative norms. Crook (1994) noted that the most obedient, the "tamest" and most compact tribes had been the strongest in early stages of human evolution, banded together by intense feelings of kinship. Darwin, initially perplexed at the place that altruism had in evolution, eventually wrote that a high standard of morality would be of little or no advantage to individual members of a tribe, but that a tribe that exhibited strong affiliation and altruism within the group would reap great benefit over other tribes without similar bonds and allegiances. (Darwin, 1871)

Recent work in sociobiology by British biologist William Hamilton presents the idea of cooperative societies operating effectively as a single organism, the result of "inclusive fitness" or the natural selection that promotes the survival and reproduction of individuals and close relatives who share much of the same genetic heritage. (Doyle, 1997) Altruism toward relatives, from this viewpoint, is not really altruism but the tendency for humans to maximize the success of their genes via their relatives, or the bodies in which copies of their genes dwell. It can be considered a sort of "nepotistic altruism". The complexity seen in any interactive human society, then, emerges, as the need for sociality and the demands of self-interest, both cultural and biological, rest in the same space. Groups, ancient and contemporary, mark their ethnic boundaries on the basis of genetically transmitted qualities (those seen in the phenotype), uniforms or adornments marking the group as distinctive from others, and from behavioral qualities such as language, conduct, or certain competencies. (van der Dennen, 1995) Benefits accrue for the individual through cooperation, but there is simultaneously a paradoxical connection to competition in the formation of ethnic groups as van der Dennen (1995) infers:

We usually think of cooperation as the opposite of competition. But if co-operation works, the evolutionary effect is to cause a kind of indirect competition with everyone else who did not cooperate quite as well.

Regardless whether one individual ever interacts with another, the two are inevitably competing in regard to which will leave more copies of its genes.

> And over the long run, those who are better at it become the ancestors of who-ever remains. In this sense, cooperation is always competition as well, and competition thus is not only inevitable but, in evolutionary terms has no alter-native. (P. 590)

Altruism, in this sense, exists in continuous tension with competition within the group and thus makes Darwinian sense as it allows for the benefits of group formation to constitute the basis on which individual competition promotes natural selection and survival of the fittest. It has been suggested that humans consider that they are a group-selected species, but perhaps it is more accurate to consider that they are "groupish", that the social organizations they form are not clearly demarcated, but rather ebb and flow and change over time, affected not so much by choice, but by environment, politics, war and aggression, and economic shifts. (Doyle, 1997)

Ingroup loyalty and outgroup emnity is, however, a persistent cross-cultural human trait. The loyalty associated with ingroup citizenship is in stark contrast to the antipathy felt and acted out on members of outgroups. Outgroup denegration might stem, at least partially, from sociobiological causes, as suggested by E.O. Wilson (1982):

> Human beings are strongly predisposed to respond with unreasoning hatred to external threats and to escalate their hostility sufficiently to overwhelm the sources of the threat by a sufficiently wide margin of safety. Our brains do appear to be programmed to the following extent: we are inclined to partition other people into friends and aliens, in the same sense that birds are inclined to learn territorial songs and to navigate by the polar constellations.
> We tend to fear deeply the actions of strangers and to solve conflicts by aggression. These learning rules are most likely to have evolved during the past hundreds of thousands of years of human evolution and, thus, to have conferred a biological advantage on those who conformed to them with the greatest fidelity. (Pp.122-123)

Fear is a primal motivator for all animals. It is programmed into animals either to run or to fly away, freeze, or adopt some kind of threat when faced with danger. (Bolles, 1970) Fear in the human is manifested in a broader spectrum of behaviors emanating from physiological reactions to threat but enlarged by cognitive capacities and language. The transient fear of strangers in infants which typically appears for several months in the latter part of the first year of life is not learned and may be part of the attachment process. Likewise in adults, the dislike of the stranger is not innate, but it does not have to be taught and can be

picked up with little help or encouragement. The human capacity for fear is exacerbated by the capacity for internally generated imagination and exaggeration
which are unique to the species. (van der Dennen, 1995)

The evolutionary program to function as a social animal, the reality of danger, and the resultant experience of fear foster separating the experienced world
into friend and foe, ingroup and outgroup.   Jean Paul Sarte wrote that "The
Other is the indispensable mediator between myself and me. I need the Other in
order to realize fully all the structures of my being." (Sarte, 1965) The "other"is
the not-me or the not-us. On this basis, given the human tendency toward self-
inflation and psychological defensive maneuvers, it becomes simple, almost
natural to denegrate "the Other".

> Ethnocentrism, according to van der Dennen (1995) is the: schismatic in-
> group/outgroup differentiation, in which internal cohesion, relative peace, soli-
> darity, loyalty and devotion to the ingroup and the glorification of the sociocen-
> tric sacred is correlated with a state of hostility or permanent quasi war toward
> outgroups which are often perceived as inferior, subhuman and/or the incorpo-
> ration of evil. Ethnocentrism results in a dualistic Manichaean morality which
> evaluates violence within the ingroup as negative, and violence against the out-
> group as positive, even desirable and heroic. (p. 446)

The sort of negative behavior that is wrought on outgroups is reinforced by
the segregation of ethnic, racial, and social groups in living and working arrangements and also by the miserly nature of human cognition. That which is
familiar tends to be embraced and that which is contradictory either ignored or
rejected. Clashing ideologies between groups provoke   cognitive discomfort
and defensiveness. Perhaps this is the result of the disturbing realization that an
opposing set of beliefs and opinions challenges the sense that one's world view
is comprehensive and certain. It unearths an upsetting vision that one's ideology
could be an arbitrary construction; that what has grounded one is perhaps largely
fictional— a personal or collective myth. Johan van der Dennen (1995) postulates
that when the ideology of one culture clashes dramatically with another that the
groups renounce the conflicting philosophy and those with whom it is associated
and demonstrate what he calls pseudospeciation. In this process, the groups ex-
aggerate both their unanimity and their difference from the "Other" to the extreme that the groups can come to see each other as completely different species,
and from this perception, the behavior toward the opposing group is accordingly
altered often in the direction of fostering violence.

Interestingly, antagonism between groups can be fostered with minimal
separation and/or ideological conflict between groups, suggesting a primal human defensive tendency. Psychological research on ingroup/outgroup behavior
has shown that groups competitive with each other where the gain of one results
in loss for the other form unfavorable stereotypes of those of the opposition
which become standardized in time. Ultimately, the outgroup is placed at a
prejudicial distance from the ingroup facilitating further enmity-building behav-

ior. (Sherif & Sherif, 1979, Noel, J.G., Wann, D. L., & Branscombe, N.R. 1995) In experimental work, this even occurred when the members of the two groups had no history of hostility, experienced no conflict of interest, did not differ in background, were matched for physical and personal characteristics, and when the reasons why the groups were formed was random and inconsequential. (Tajfel & Turner, 1979, Smith, 1992, van der Dennen, 1995). It was further demonstrated that the existence of the outgroup and increasing competitive and aggressive feelings toward them enhances cooperation and democracy within the ingroup, making it function more effectively. (Sherif & Sherif, 1979)

The distrust and fear between groups generated from the processes of ethnocentrism is complimented in a negative sense by xenophobia and paranoia. In terms of survival, it is perhaps adaptive for a society to avoid destruction by outsiders by developing a generalized tendency to distrust strangers. This thinking would suggest that one incident of misplaced trust could be fatal so an all-encompassing tendency to fear and rebuke outsiders works effectively as a protective albeit neurotic strategy. In justifying aggression, mildly paranoid thinking could be adaptive in a highly competitive situation as it uncomplicates the mind, envisioning home as good and away as evil and gratifies self esteem in transferring responsibility for behavior from oneself to another. The defensive mechanisms of projection and denial can lessen cognitive dissonance and in a general sense simplify a complicated, unsettling emotional situation. (Barash & Lipton, 1985)

In considering the origins of war, the natural tendency toward groupishness needs to be fueled by competition and aggression in order to be realized. Konrad Lorenz and Sigmund Freud both asserted that aggression was innate. Lorenz argued that aggression is critical in species preservation in that it promotes survival of the fittest, achieves spacing and population control and strengthens the pair-bond by shared aggression against competitors. (Lorenz, 1974) Freud's notions of the innateness of the sex and aggression drives color much of his theory. Dramatic contemporary research on electrical and chemical stimulation of the brain creates the basis for the belief that aggression is a biologically-based entity. (Goldstein, 1989) It has been demonstrated that males are more likely to injure or kill other humans than are females and that humans are most likely to harm others at the stage in life when they are most likely to reproduce. Closely related people tend to have more similar aggressive styles than more distantly related people and much of this patterning and organization appears without being obviously learned, supporting aggression as an innate tendency in humans. (Bateson, 1989)

Aggression in groups against an enemy is largely a human design. Although animals are typically social, with a wide variety of natural groupings, it is rare for one group to attack another, particularly of its own species. Lorenz noted there there is an inhibition that predators such as wolves or hawks tend to possess against using their natural lethal weapons against their own species. (Lorenz, 1974) Although it would seem most logical, especially from a human perspective, to extinguish one's enemies, often when animals set out to fight it is more of a demonstration of threat or strength than a setting for murder. Threat and bluff are typical and gestures of surrender are recognized by victors who tend, at that point, to refrain from the final killing blow. (Dawkins, 1989) There is a human parallel to this behavior which reflects aggression but ultimately is non-violent. Anthropologists have long written of the flexibility and cultural relativity of aggression. For example, certain Eskimo people settle their conflicts by singing abusive songs about their enemies. Indians of Santa Marta strike a tree or rock with sticks instead of hitting each other; the first one to break his stick was considered the braver and hence the victor. (Goldstein, 1989) Although we share a biological heritage through evolution, there is an array of behaviors distinctly available to the human around aggression relating to our cognitive and language skills and the fact that people, in their upbringing, are exposed to a complex set of rewards and punishments, beliefs and traditions, which mold behavior and affect when and how humans battle with each other both individually and in groups. (Huntingford, 1989)

Although the human is not alone in the animal world in showing a capability of killing its own species, it is perhaps unique in the frightening scale at which it has done so. Most animal fights take place between pairs of animals and not groups. In many successful species, flocks, herds, schools, form, merge and break up to the mutual benefit of all concerned and with little or no aggression. (Huntingford, 1989) The way in which humans have come to separate themselves out from other groups and cast others of their own kind as enemies helps create a unique style of warfare and same-species destruction that is unprecedented in the animal world.

Fighting in groups requires coalition-forming and thus a certain level of cognitive ability. The only other species that have been seen to conduct this sort of combat are chimpanzees as seen through the work of Jane Goodall. Scientific analysis has revealed that humans and chimpanzees are more closely related than originally thought, having descended from a common ancestor that inhabited east Africa in the late Miocene era, approximately eight million years ago. Homosapiens and Pan troglodytes seem to be the only two species in which males form coalitions within the group (instead of fighting as is common in other species) and plan and carried out lethal hostilities against other groups of the same species. (Doyle, 1997)

The chimp warfare resembles a raiding party rather than the sort of full-blown conflict we associate with human warfare. Goodall observed a great eagerness in young prime male chimpanzees for the behaviors involved in male raiding parties, but she also points out quite emphatically that there are distinct individual differences. (van der Dennan, 1995) The greater cognizance and reflectivity of chimps when compared to other animals reflects a similarity to the human, that under the same circumstance, certain individuals are keen for conflict and others are averse to the violence. At the same time, the similarities between the chimp raiding parties and human war can only be stretched so far. There is little in the animal kingdom that is directly comparable to the scale of human warfare and nothing that is analogous to contemporary international warfare. (Huntingford, 1989)

Humans organize themselves in much larger in groups than can be found in the animal world. Given this, new forms of social control have evolved to ensure ingroup cooperation, as kin altruism could not function on a large scale. A morality system came to be incorporated into the various societal schemes of nations in the interest of maintaining stability. Roele (1993) explains:

> If the size of societies increases, the basis for altruism erodes and the enactment of a (religiously inspired) system of morality becomes necessary. The system of morality would require individuals to help their neighbors and act in the common interest and would aim to reduce intragroup competition, especially reproductive competition, e.g. by means of socially imposed monogamy, but possibly also by fomenting intergroup competition; such a system of morality is an ideal one for exploitation, indoctrination and disciplinization of young males in standing armies and warlike exploits. (p. 593)

Indeed, notions of ingroup "good" and outgroup "evil" can be constructed and fortified by religion, morality systems, and government. Emotional contagion, in addition, can unite a formerly fragmented group of individuals. The moral/emotional cauldron of self-righteous connection with a nation state and defamation of particular others serves the "interests" of governments well.

Nations cannot hate and enmify others, only individuals can, and thus there must be a psychological process of enemy-making that functions at the individual level which can eventually be spread at a group level. Freud and his contemporary post-Freudian psychologists, many of whom lived through World War I in Europe, were appalled at the bloody violence seen at a scale never before experienced in history. Freud asserted that much of the inhumanity and violence of wartime had to do with the operation of Thanatos, or the death instinct which for him operated in opposition to Eros, the life instinct. He suggested that when Thanatos was thwarted by Eros, its energy was displaced outward, causing aggression between individuals and groups. He noted that a "civilized society" needed to repress both of these instincts in the interest of cooperation and that the repression of such powerful, raw instincts in humans produces neurosis, discontent, and ultimately further disorder. (Barash& Webel, 2002)

Alfred Adler, who followed Freud, considered that the human was capable of developing empathy and altruism, in his words, "social interest," without necessarily having to deal with the uncomfortable repression of the life and death instincts. For Adler, neurotic individuals who lacked social feeling easily acquired enemies and this individual characteristic also manifested itself in warlike nations. (Rieber, 1991; Parrott, 1997) Carl Jung also looked to the "dark side" of the psyche in explaining war, contending that in times of political disorder when the unifying myths of society disintegrate, the stage is set for fresh eruptions of material from the collective unconscious. (Rieber, 1991). Jung reflects on his notions of the origin of the behaviors that led to the slaughter which was "The Great War":

> The war forces upon the attention of every thinking person the problem of the chaotic unconscious which slumbers uneasily beneath the ordered world of consciousness. This war has pitilessly revealed to civilized man that he is still a barbarian, and has at the same time shown what an iron scourge lies in store for him if ever again he should be tempted to make his neighbor responsible for his own evil qualities. (Jung, 1972)

Jung refers in this quotation to the conflict inherent between the persona and the shadow. In the interest of the preservation of positive self-appraisal, it is common, according to Jung, for an individual to identify too strongly with the virtue associated with one's social roles, represented as the persona, the aspect of the individual which is shown to the world. This perceived virtue cloaks those areas of the self that have been rejected or repressed and which exist as the unconscious shadow. For Jung, if the shadow is unacknowledged it is seen in the form of projections in the conscious world. (Whitmont, 1991) This theory would suggest that the construction of "enemy" often has much to do with projected images of rejected aspects of the human psyche. David Barash (1994) speaks to this:

> By clutching our enemies, we avoid self awareness. We see, clearly enough – and hate, readily enough – the hideous, leering vulture that gnaws daily at our liver, but we fail to see our own face. And so, like Diogenes the Cynic, we search the streets at night, holding aloft our lantern and projecting our shadows everywhere, startled from time to time by the shifting apparitions of our own making, looking desperately for what we dare not find inside ourselves. (p. 98)

The projected "dark side" is seen in much of psychoanalytic thought and is reinforced by cultural, religious, and political dogma across cultures. The constructions of "good" and "evil" as concrete concepts make short work of enemy-making both on an individual and a group level. Deconstructing this concreteness makes simple projections more difficult. Chu Hsi, an ancient Chinese philosopher, taught that good and evil have no existence in themselves but are terms applied to things according to their advantage or injury to oneself or to humankind. "Nature itself," Chu Hsi taught, "is beyond good and evil and ignores our egoistic terminology." (Sanford, 1981) Shakespeare's Hamlet similarly comments to Rosencrantz, "There is nothing either good or bad, but thinking makes it so." Jung also acknowledged the relativity of good and evil. He warned against considering them exact opposites, of the simple view that good has a clear imperative and evil can be shunned. "Recognition of the reality of evil necessarily relativizes the good, and the evil likewise, converting both into halves of a paradoxical whole." (Jung, 1991, p. 171.) For Jung, awareness came through self-knowledge which meant to him the utmost possible knowledge of one's wholeness.

He must know relentlessly how much good he can do, and what crimes he is capable of, and must beware of regarding the one as real and the other and the other as illusion. Both are elements within his nature, and both are bound to come to light in him, should he wish – as he ought – to live without self deception or self delusion. (Jung, 1991, p. 172)

It is difficult to speculate whether "one's wholeness" can be known. This knowledge is certainly subject to tenacious preventative efforts of individual defense mechanisms which protect the individual from psychic discomfort. Considering nation as organism, the dark side of a civilization is carefully protected from public scrutiny on a myriad of levels through government organizations and mass media. The ruling body tries to present itself and the people it represents as virtuous and very often points outside to enemies who represent "evil." Charismatic leaders can create militaristic fervor and emotional contagion in a people who believe in the propaganda they confront daily. At its extreme, under very special and specific circumstances, a situation like World War II Germany can emerge. The extremes to which one of the most civilized and educated populations on earth went in the pursuit of glory following a charismatic leader could not have been anticipated until they were experienced. Extreme distortions of reality, including the process of reification where "ideas become real," referring to the potential to treat an abstraction as an actual thing, were required and used. It can even be anthropomorphized, taking on a human or human-like form, a familiar example being the abstract concept of "evil" becoming the "devil".

Other examples would be propaganda that creates personal images of the "motherland" or the "fatherland" promoted by fervent speeches and patriotic pamphlets, rituals, flags, songs, demonstrations and other tools which are highly effective in promoting group solidarity, as they make the frightening, unknown, and chaotic outcomes of aggression and violence seem familiar and more safe. The successful transformation of a country into something that feels like a family or kin unit can be particularly effective in mobilizing support. It seems that the "remarkable propensity of people for projecting part of their individual self-love into specific social units, to which they are linked by strong feelings of identity and of belonging, is one of the roots of the dangers which human groups constitute for each other." (van der Dennen, 1995 p.480) This seemed to be accurate for World War II Germany with Hitler fitting the role of an unconflicted cult leader with a malleable collection of followers who demonstrated absolute loyalty to him amid constant inflammation of the cause of the "fatherland". It is obvious that his ceaseless message exemplified the enhancement of his Aryan "ingroup" and the denegration of outsiders who were portrayed as inferior on most conceivable levels. Inflaming ingroup loyalty and militant emotion to a very high pitch, fortified by a sense of moral correctness, can cause and has caused many individuals to literally "lose their minds" in the sense that they betray reason and willingly sacrifice themselves for a cause that, upon reflection, would not be worthy of such a sacrifice. "Men and women first construct

towering structures of theology and religion, complex analyses of racial character and class structure, or moralities of group life and virility before they kill one
another . . . Men will die like flies for theories and exterminate each other with
every instrument of destruction for abstractions." (Durbin & Bowlby, 1938 in
van der Dennen, 1995) Unconflicted leaders such as Hitler fuel their followers
with passionate nationalistic rhetoric and speak with assurance about "good and
evil," directing action against outside agents or groups with confidence and cer-
titude.

Using the Hitler image, although the country was emotionally swept up in
Nazi fervor, it is difficult to imagine the processes by which seemingly normal
soldiers allow themselves to commit atrocities. Guards in the Nazi death camps
believed they were being model citizens when they sent countless Jews, eastern
Europeans, and others to their deaths. It seems that sadism was not the main
cause for the horrifying violence, but perhaps conformity pressures:

> It is not the murderers, the criminals, the delinquents, and the wild noncon-
> formists who have embarked on the really significant rampages of killing, tor-
> ture and mayhem. Rather it is the conformist, virtuous citizens, acting in the
> name of righteous causes and intensely held beliefs who throughout history
> have perpetuated the fiery holocausts of war, the religious persecutions, the
> sacks of cities, the wholesale rape of women, the dismemberment of the old
> and the young and other unspeakable horrors . . . The crimes of violence com-
> mitted for selfish, personal motives are historically insignificant compared to
> those committed ad majorem gloriam Dei, out of a self-sacrificing devotion to
> flag, a leader, a religious faith, or a political conviction. Man has always been
> prepared not only to kill but also to die for good, bad, or completely futile
> causes. (Koestler, 1967)

Perhaps the processes at work in this self-destructive pattern of behavior
where excessive conformity or loyalty wreak havoc has much to do with the
human imagination's capacity, with emotional incitement, to embrace an
unlikely paradise myth or Utopian doctrine and to allow it to supercede a ra-
tional and sane sense of things.

Freud saw nationalistic dynamics in the context of a family structure and set
the drama in the light of the Oedipus complex. What was key in creating un-
questioning loyalty to country was the identity with the leader, a substitute for
the father. This common identification with a familial, hierarchical figure
formed the basis for group cohesion and identity. Aggression against the leader,
the flip side of the original Oedipal ambivalence toward the father, became ta-
boo and had to be discharged against outsiders. (Rieber, 1991) Konrad Lorenz,
rooting the basis of aggression to a more instinctual biological origin in the human, was, however, in agreement with Freud in acknowledging the danger of
militant enthusiasm in enhancing the likelihood that people would lose their
normal inhibitions against violence when united with others who were similarly
motivated. (Lorenz, 1974)

Emotional contagion, militant enthusiasm, the projection of evil outward, though illogical and inaccurate, can clearly work to the political advantage of a country. Charles DeGaulle once noted, " a nation does not have friends; it has only interests." (Rieber, 1991) Outgroup denigration has been used by leaders through history to maximize group "interests." Though illogical, this projection of evil outward and the resultant scapegoating can be productive toward desired political ends. Freud noted that hatred against a person or institution operates in a unifying way and could possibly result in the same kind of emotional ties as positive attachment. (Freud, 1921) When the lion is at the door, seemingly insignificant differences are put aside in the interest of survival. The sort of social conflict that unites a disparate group seems to work so long as the threatening patterns are crisscrossing and do not repeatedly fracture at the same place. (Barash, 1994, Beck 1999) Republicans and Democrats, Catholics and Baptists, African Americans and Caucasians, can unite against a larger threat that seeks to thwart them as long as it does not irritate the sore points that traditionally separate these groups.

Absolute notions of "good and evil" are common in political rhetoric. Communism, and the Soviet Union as arch-enemy, were vilified through the McCarthy era, the Vietnam War, and into the eighties when the USSR collapsed under its own weight. Even Richard Nixon, who took pride in his ability in foreign affairs, an ability which was widely acknowledged, was capable of employing immense simplification to suit his ends. When Ronald Reagan was running for president, Nixon stated:: "It may seem melodramatic to say that the U.S. and Russia [sic] represent Good and Evil, Light and Darkness, God and the Devil. But if we think of it that way, it helps to clarify our perspective of the world struggle." (Nixon, 1980). Reagan famously termed the Soviet Union "The Evil Empire;" later, George W. Bush warned of an "Axis of Evil" comprised of Iran, Iraq, and North Korea. Hardly "axis:" Iran and Iraq have a history of mortal enmity and North Korea is an isolated nation with little contact with the rest of the world.

Simplistic notions of good and evil associated with religious belief can also give fuel to the enmification of an outgroup. If one is on "God's side," much can be justified. When one is up against Satan and the forces of evil, there is no reason to expect a fair fight and hence no reason to fight fairly oneself. (Baumeister, 1997) Fundamentalism in many religions has given rise to the justification of the destruction of the unsaved or the infidels. The separation of God and Satan, heaven and hell (and earth), reinforces the concept of the existence of pure evil for the religious, and the notion of original sin found in some Christian sects encourages retaliation against projections of the shadow in the form of other humans who represent that which groups or individuals despise in themselves. It is interesting that in other belief systems such as Greek mythology and Native American creeds, there is no clear separation between a God of pure "good" and an opposing Satanic being of "evil." "Only among the Greeks was there no war among the gods (quarrels, maybe, but no wars), for these gods and goddesses were too wise to claim to be good." (Sanford, 1981, p. 23) There was no god in Greek mythology to whom is ascribed the origin of all good things, rather each of the gods is capable of both good and evil. Native Americans were perplexed at the Christian notion of a satanic being for they felt that human beings reflected nature in embodying both the "good" and the "bad," the beneficent and the cruel. To represent their belief in the dual nature of humankind, they often painted their faces white on one side and black on the other for religious ceremonial purposes. (Sanford, 1981)

Jung said, "I would rather be whole than good". (Miller, 1991) The danger of holding on to pretenses of goodness is that such pretenses deny access to important albeit unwelcome information about individual or collective flaws. It could be argued that America is vulnerable to a certain paranoia in its politics stemming directly from this condition. The mythology of America, from the perspective of our European "founders," is that this is a land established on a philosophy of fairness and tolerance to all. The symbolism on the back of a dollar bill expresses this philosophy quite clearly. The pyramid on the left of the bill starts with four points at the bottom (as the four points of the compass) which move upward, ultimately joining at the top in the eye, the knowing eye of God, which is a meeting point and place available to those who seek. At the bottom are two inscriptions in Latin, *"Novus Ordo Seclorum"* ("A New Order of the World") and *"Annuit Coeptis,"* ("He has smiled on our accomplishments."). Behind the pyramid is a desert and in front of it, plants are growing symbolizing moving away from the chaos, war, and disorder of Europe to a new, fertile, promising beginning. The eagle on the right is the bird of Zeus, the principle of deity. In one of his talons, the eagle holds thirteen arrows which symbolize the principle of war. In the other, a laurel wreath with thirteen leaves symbolizes the principle of peace; not without meaning the eagle gazes in the direction of the laurel wreath. (Campbell, 1988) This symbolism represents the hope of America at its founding and includes the field of opposites. The new country looked back at its bleak European roots and sought to create a new culture founded on fairness and reason. Although the individuals in the "melting pot" came from scattered points on the compass and varied backgrounds, they could ascend and seek unity and wisdom as symbolized by the "eye" of God. The eagle acknowledges the dark side of war with the arrows in its talon, but chooses the way of peace in its gaze toward the laurel wreath. Keeping the dark and the light in view, so beautifully articulated on the dollar, suggests balance. Taking the idealism from the founders, disregarding the clearly defined dangers, and expounding only on the virtues of America, throws the human system out of balance. It promotes a sense of specialness, a sense of superiority that makes America vulnerable to criticism and very capable of demonizing others who threaten her treasured self-image. (Barash 1994)

There is a special danger in the manner in which this paranoia plays out in the post-Soviet era. The United States, now the sole superpower in the world, has no enemies of the sort known in the 20th century, countries whose military and economic strength could realistically threaten the existence of the U.S.

David Barash speaks of the enemy system being similar to a codependent, in that their life focuses on the relationship with the other. If a codependent's other heals and does not need the aid and support required previously, the codependent loses an important role in life. (Barash, 1994) Even in a less neurotic frame of reference, contemplating Sarte's reflection that he needed the "other" to know who he was, what does one do when there is no comparable "other?" What does a country used to reacting to adversaries do when they go away?

In the decade when the Soviet Union was waning as a imminent threat, the threat of the Muslim "other" was rising. The hostage crisis in Iran gave rise to very public denegrations moving in both directions between the U.S. and Iran, then led by Ayatollah Khomeini. Moammar Khaddafi in Libya was a targeted enemy in the 80s and was ultimately eclipsed by Saddam Hussein and Osama bin Laden. The North/South global inequalities mirror the view disseminated in much of the world press that violence is either carried out between Southern countries or against Northern interests and that, given this rich/poor context, Muslim violence is the worst sort of terrorism as it is seen as opposing modernity and technologically advanced countries with barbaric extremism stemming from a history of fanaticism. (Chomsky, 1992) Because the North controls international communication networks, this misrepresention is the way that most of the world is guided to perceive the Muslim. (Karim, 1997) Events in the 21st century seem to reinforce the view that the growing "otherness" of the Muslim world is providing the neurotic context in which the U.S. and others can frame themselves as upholding freedom against a dark and dangerous foe, and thus justify aggressive, self-interested behavior.

This essay has focused on psychological and sociobiological notions of the "natural" progression of the human toward modern warfare. It is incomplete if it does not consider the multi-disciplinary evidence that supports the notion that group aggressive tendencies are not inevitable. Actual experience in combat suggests an aversion to killing other humans. During World War II, for example, rarely more than 25% of soldiers fired their guns in battle even in the most heated of engagements. (Barash & Webel, 2002) A study sponsored by the U.S. Army at the time concluded that "it is therefore reasonable to believe that the average and healthy individual—the man who can endure the mental and physical stresses of combat—still has such an inner and usually unrealized resistance towards killing a fellow man that he will not of his own volition take life if it is possible to turn away from that responsibility." (Barash & Webel, 2002, p. 139) After exhaustively interviewing many combat veterans of World War II, U. S. Army General S.L.A. Marshall concluded that the "primary motivation for individual US servicemen to fire their guns during battle was not fear for their own lives, or patriotism, or desire to help end the war, or hatred of the enemy but rather the potent feeling of solidarity with a small group of buddies." (Barash, 1994, p. 68) Largely due to these findings, military training changed following World War II and the percentage of soldiers willing to fire their weapons during the Korean and Vietnam wars increased as a result of more intense training, a more physically distant enemy as war technology changed, and also because of an emphasis on ingroup solidarity. (Barash & Webel, 2002)

Sociobiology has been called the science that pretends that people cannot talk. (Doyle, 1997) The potentials of written and spoken language and the cognitive capacities they represent provide a broader array of potentials for the human than can be seen in the lives of animal ancestors. The Seville Statement, which was drafted by a distinguished group of social and natural scientists from around the world in 1986, was adopted by UNESCO in 1989. The statement contends that war is not an tendency inherited from our animal ancestors, that violent behavior is not programmed into human nature, that humans do not have "violent brains" and that war is not caused by instinct or any single motivation. It concludes: "The same species who invented war is capable of inventing peace." (http://www.unesco.org/human_rights/hrtv.htm).

Free will regarding the will to war is espoused, although differently, by giants in associated fields of the social sciences. Sociologist Emile Durkheim contended that social phenomena have to be explained in relation to other social phenomena and so it is seen that almost any behaviors can become stable in groups if they are reinforced by social norms. (Doyle, 1997) Anthropologist Margaret Mead argued that warfare was an invention of human societies where they send their young men out to pursue any number of self serving interests and goals. Since it is an invention, warfare, when it becomes outmoded or self-destructive, can be altered by the same processes that created it. (Mead, 2000) Even Sigmund Freud, in a correspondence with fellow pacifist Albert Einstein, espoused the belief that war was avoidable. Freud considered war odious, an assault on human integrity, in that "every man has a right over his own life, and war destroys lives that were full of promise; forces the individual into situations that shame his manhood, obliging him to murder fellow men against his will; it ravages material amenities, the fruits of human toil, and much besides." (p. 12) He suggested that the solution to overcoming the primitive aggressive instincts he discussed could come through the strengthening of the intellect and the introversion of the aggressive impulse which he felt would bring about both benefit and peril. (Freud, 2000). Jung's "feeling function" is the internal mechanism of the psyche that helps the human determine the value of elements of life free of egocentric concerns. It gives guidance regarding that which is desirable or not desirable, and thus can be valuable in making ethical judgments such as those around war and peace. Some suggest that the feeling function ultimately was the force, for example, which turned much of the American public against the Vietnam War. Despite the fact that demonstrations to stop the war were unprecedented in this country and for many were "unpatriotic," and the fact that they opposed what were supposedly our political aims, and, ultimately, the concept that the war was a political maneuver that was simply "wrong" emerged for many. With accurate information, the feeling function of the human psyche is able, perhaps even designed, to come to accurate conclusions in situations where a moral decision is appropriate. (Miller, 1991) Giving permission to go to war, or to refrain from so doing, is one of those decisions, considering the fact that its outcomes are always very damaging in some respect no matter what one's view of a "good" outcome is.

Konrad Lorenz (1974) specifically cited four interlocking processes that were associated with the willingness of a group to decide to go to war against another group. Lorenz's formula for war-making by an ethnic or nation state is an inspiring leader communicating a danger from the outside which ultimately generates militant enthusiasm against a hated enemy shared by other individuals similarly agitated. He reflects back on the roots of this militant enthusiasm by evoking images of the male chimpanzee defending his band or family with self-sacrificing courage and a set of threatening gestures to the outsider. He feels that the unthinking single-mindedness of this response must have been of high survival value even in a tribe of fully evolved human beings. Although this biological evolution is perhaps the root of our mistrust of outside groups, it does not address accurately the scope of human potential regarding war and enemy-making. Lorenz's processes are highly emotional, exploiting a primal fear of the unknown. To the extent that it is then a human construction, it can be addressed and overridden with forces of feeling and mind unavailable to animals.

Conclusion

Expanding the notion of human potential is necessary in order to have a fuller idea of our options related to forming a peaceful global community. One might consider that the processes of our evolution go beyond the biological and are additionally spiritual and intellectual, and thus distinctively human. Cultural evolution, with written and spoken language, moves at a much more rapid pace than biological evolution; globalization with all its accompanying problems simultaneously offers an array of new opportunity in that the tribes of the human are increasingly interconnected. Knowledge, communication, and technology are enlarging and elaborating at a previously unknown pace, propelling us into a place previously unknown. There is a wide range of opinion regarding whether we are declining rapidly and perhaps irreversibly toward global environmental or political catastrophe, or whether our crises are leading us toward a favorable future. Crisis precedes transformation; when a limitation is reached, nature does not necessarily adapt and stabilize, but innovates and transforms. Problems are often evolutionary drivers vital to transformation. (Hubbard, 1998) As Joseph Campbell noted, what is needed is perhaps a "planetary myth," a uniting story that creates a global ingroup as our interconnectedness swiftly increases and the uniting threats of destruction mount for all people. The challenge is one that requires a sophisticated human cognitive and emotional effort of a greater magnitude than that which created contemporary crises. The research, methodology, and wisdom inherent in this transformation are available to our global culture. Let us resolve to seek them.

Works Cited

Barash, D. P. *Beloved Enemies: Our Need for Opponents* New York:Prometheus Books., 1994.

Barash, D. P. & Lipton, J. E. *The Caveman and the Bomb: Human Nature, Evolution, and Nuclear War.* New York: McGraw-Hill, 1985.

Barash, D. P. & Webel, C. *Peace and Conflict Studies.* Thousand Oaks, California: Sage Publications, 2002.

Bateson, P. "Is aggression instinctive?" In Groebel, J. & Hinde, R. (eds.), *Aggression and War: Their Biological and Social Bases* (pp. 35-47). Cambridge, England: University Press, 1989.

Baumeister, R. F. *Evil: Inside Human Violence and Cruelty.* New York: W. H. Freeman and Company, 1996.

Beck, A. T. *Prisoners of Hate: The Cognitive Basis of Anger, Hostility and Violence.* New York: HarperCollins Publishers Inc, 1999.

Bolles, R. C. "Species-specific defense reactions and avoidance learning" *Psychological Review,* 77, 1970, pp. 32-48.

Campbell, J. and Moyers, B., Eds. *The Power of Myth.* New York: Random House Inc.,1988.

Chomsky, N. *Deterring democracy.* New York: Hill & Wang, 1992.

Crook, P. *Darwinism, War and History: the Debate over the Biology of War from the 'Origin of Species' to the First World War.* New York: Cambridge University Press, 1994.

Darwin, C. *The Descent of Man.* Amherst, New York: Promethius Books, 1871.

Dawkins, R. *The Selfish Gene.* Oxford, England: Oxford University Press, 1989.

Doyle, D. "The Origins of War: Biological and Anthropological Theories." *History and Theory* 35, 1996, pp. 1-28.

Doyle, D. "Evolutionary theory and group selection: the question of warfare." *History and Theory* 38, no. 4, 1999, pp. 79-100.

Freud, S. "Group Psychology and Analysis of the Ego." *Standard Edition of the Complete Psychological Works of Sigmund Freud.* London: Hogarth Press, 1921.

_____. "Why War?" Barash, D., Ed. *Approaches to Peace, A Reader in Peace Studies.* New York: Oxford University Press, 1959, pp/ 9-13.

Goldstein, J. H. "Beliefs About Human Aggression." Groebel, J. & Hinde, R., Eds. *Aggression and War: Their Biological and Social* Bases. Cambridge, England: University Press, 1989, pp. 10-19.

Hubbard, B. M. *Conscious Evolution.* Novato, California: New World Library, 1998..

Huntingford, F. A. "Animals fight, but do not make war." Groebel, J. & Hinde, R., Eds. *Aggression and War: Their Biological and Social Bases.* Cambridge, England: University Press, 1989, pp. 25-34.

Jung, C. *Two Essays on Analytical Psychology.* Princeton: Bollingen Press, 1972.

_____. "The Problem of Evil Today." Zweig, C. & Abrams, J., Eds. *Meeting the Shadow: The Hidden Power of the Dark Side of Human Nature* New York: Penguin Putnam Inc, 1991, pp. 170-173.

Karim, H. K."Core Images of the Muslim Other." Riggins, S. H., Ed.*The Language and Politics of Exclusion - Others in Discourse* (pp. 174-177).London: Sage Publications, 1997, pp. 174-177.

Koestler, R. *The Ghost in the Machine.* London: Pan Books, 1967.

Lorenz, K. *On Aggression.* San Diego, California: Harcourt Brace & Co, 1974.

Mead. M. "Warfare is Only an Invention – Not a Biological Necessity." Barash, D., Ed. *Approaches to Peace, A Reader in Peace Studies* (pp. 19-22). New York: Oxford University Press, pp. 19-22.

Miller, W. "Finding the Shadow in Daily Life." Zweig, C. & Abrams, J., Eds. *Meeting the Shadow: The Hidden Power of the Dark Side of Human Nature* New York: Penguin Putnam Inc, 1991, pp. 38-44.

Nixon, R. "America has Slipped to Number Two." *Parade Magazine.* October 5, 1980.

Noel, J.G., Wann, D. L., & Branscombe, N.R. "Peripheral Ingroup Membership Status and Public Negativity Toward Outgroups." *Journal of Personality and Social Psychology* 68, No. 1, 1995, pp 127-137.

Parrott, L. *Counseling and Psychotherapy.* New York: McGraw-Hill, 1997.

Rieber, R. *The Psychology of War and Peace: The Image of the Enemy.* New York: Plenum Press, 1991.

Roele, M. "Religious behaviour as a utility- and inclusive fitness-optimizing strategy." *Social Science Info.,* 32,3, 1993, pp. 387-417

Ross, M. H. "The role of evolution in ethnocentric conflict and its management." *Journal of Social Issues* 47, No. 1,1991, pp. 167-185.

Sanford, J. *Evil: The Shadow Side of Reality.* New York: The Crossroad Publishing Co, 2001.

Sarte, J.P.and Cumming, R., Eds. *The Philosophy of Jean-Paul Sarte.* New York: Random House, 1965.

Seville Statement on Violence, Spain (1986). Retrieved January 13, 2003, from http://www.unesco.org/human_rights/hrtv.html.

Sherif, M. & Sherif, C. "Research on Intergroup Relations." Austin, W. & Worchel, S., Eds. *The Social Psychology of Intergroup Relations* (pp. 10-15). Monterey, California: Brooks/Cole Publishing Co, 1979.

Smith, M. B. "Nationalism, Ethnocentrism, and the New World Order." *Journal of Humanistic Psychology* 32, No. 4.1993, pp. 76-91.

Tajfel, H. & Turner, J. "An Integrative Theory of Intergroup Conflict." In Austin, W. & Worchel, S., Eds. *The Social Psychology of Intergroup Relations* (pp. 34-36). Monterey, California: Brooks/Cole Publishing Co, 1979, pp. 34-36.

van der Dennen, J. M. G. *The Origin of War: The Evolution of a Male-Coalitional Reprodcutive Strategy.* Groningen, The Netherlands: Origin Press, 1995.

Whitmont, E. C. "The Evolution of the Shadow." Zweig, C. & Abrams, J., Eds. *Meeting the Shadow: The Hidden Power of the Dark Side of Human Nature* New York: Penguin Putnam Inc, 1991, pp. 12-19.

Wilson, E. O. *On Human Nature.* New York: Bantam Books, 1982.

Index

About the Contributors

Marie A. Conn, Professor of Religious Studies, holds a PhD from the University of Notre Dame.

Nancy DeCesare, IHM, Assistant Professor of Sociology, holds a PhD from New York University.

Sara Kitchen, Associate Professor of Sociology, holds a JD from the Law School of Villanova University.

Barbara Lonnquist, Associate Professor of English, holds a PhD from the University of Pennsylvania.

Thérèse McGuire, SSJ, Associate Professor of Art, holds a PhD from New York University.

Nancy Porter, Associate Professor of Psychology, holds a PhD from the University of Pennsylvania.

Margie Thompson, SSJ, Associate Professor of Art, holds an MFA from the Moore College of Art.

www.ingramcontent.com/pod-product-compliance
Lightning Source LLC
Chambersburg PA
CBHW020356270326
41926CB00007B/463